THEMATIC UNIT
Mice

Written by Fran Van Vorst

Teacher Created Materials, Inc.
6421 Industry Way
Westminster, CA 92683
www.teachercreated.com
©2000 Teacher Created Materials, Inc.
Made in U.S.A.

ISBN-1-57690-365-6

Illustrated by
Bruce Hedges

Edited by
Janet A. Hale, M.S. Ed.

Cover Art by
Cheri Macoubrie Wilson

Table of Contents

Introduction

Mice is a captivating, comprehensive, 80-page thematic unit designed to immerse children in writing, poetry, language arts, science, math, social studies, music, art, and life skills. The literature and activities used in this thematic unit have been selected to help children gain a better understanding about mice. In addition, children will experience working cooperatively, being considerate of others, and taking into consideration another's point of view. A variety of teaching strategies such as cooperative learning, hands-on experiences, and child-centered assessment are integrated throughout the unit.

This thematic unit includes the following:

- ❏ **literature selections**—summaries of two children's books with related lessons (complete with reproducible pages) that cross the curriculum

- ❏ **poetry**—suggested selections and lessons enabling children to write and publish their own works

- ❏ **choral expression**—to encourage children to participate in groups

- ❏ **planning guides**—suggestions for sequencing your lesson plans

- ❏ **writing ideas**—daily suggestions as well as across-the-curriculum writing activities

- ❏ **research topics**—to develop the ability to organize and report on various subjects

- ❏ **bulletin-board ideas**—suggestions and plans for child-created and/or interactive bulletin boards

- ❏ **comparing and contrasting**—to encourage children to develop critical evaluation

- ❏ **surveys and graphing**—to mathematically extend the theme

- ❏ **curriculum connections**—in language arts, math, science, social studies, art, choral expression, drama, and life skills

- ❏ **culminating activities**—to synthesize learning and to produce a product or engage in an activity that can be shared with others

- ❏ **a bibliography**—suggesting additional fiction and nonfiction books, as well as other helpful resources

> **To keep this valuable resource intact so that it can be used year after year, you may wish to punch holes in the pages and store them in a three-ring binder.**

Introduction (cont.)

Why a Balanced Approach?

The strength of a balanced language approach is that it involves children in using all modes of communication—reading, writing, listening, illustrating, and doing. Communication skills are interconnected and integrated into lessons that emphasize the whole of language. Implicit in this approach is our knowledge that every whole—including individual words—is composed of parts, and directed study of those parts can help a child to master the whole. Experience and research tell us that regular attention to phonics, other word attack skills, spelling, etc., develops reading mastery, thereby fulfilling the unity of the whole language experience. The child is thus led to read, write, spell, speak, and listen confidently in response to a literature experience introduced by the teacher. In these ways, language skills grow rapidly, stimulated by direct practice, involvement, and interest in the topic.

Why Thematic Planning?

One very useful tool for implementing an integrated whole language program is thematic planning. By choosing a theme with correlating literature selections for a unit of study, a teacher can plan activities throughout the day that lead to a cohesive, in-depth study of the topic. Children will be practicing and applying their skill in meaningful contexts. Consequently, they will tend to learn and retain more. Both teachers and children will be freed from a day that is broken into unrelated segments of isolated drill and practice.

Why Cooperative Learning?

Besides academic skills and content, children need to learn social skills. No longer can this area of development be neglected or be taken for granted. Children need to learn to work cooperatively in groups in order to function in modern society. Group activities should be a regular part of school life and teachers should consciously include social objectives as well as academic objectives in their planning. For example, a group working together to write a report may need to select a leader. The teacher should make it clear to the children about the leader's position and monitor the leader-follower group interaction just as he or she would do with the basic goals of the project.

Why Big Books?

An excellent cooperative, whole language activity is the production of big books. Groups of children, or the whole classroom can apply their language skills, content, knowledge, and creativity to produce a big book that can become a part of the classroom library and may be read and reread during free-reading sessions. These books make excellent culminating projects for sharing beyond the classroom with parents, librarians, other classes, etc.

Why Journals?

Each day your children should have the opportunity to write in a journal. They may respond to a book or an event in history, write about a personal experience, or answer a general "question of the day" posed by the teacher. The culminative journal provides an excellent means of documenting a child's writing progress.

If You Give a Mouse a Cookie

by Laura Joffe Numeroff

Summary

If You Give a Mouse a Cookie *is a comical story of a mouse, a small boy, and an adventure in giving. Once the mouse is offered a cookie, it seems its requests never end. Exhausted by all the activity, the boy needs to take a rest . . . but what if the mouse asks again for a glass of milk—you know he'll ask for another cookie. . . .*

The outline below is a suggested plan for using the various activities presented in this unit. You can adapt these ideas to fit your own classroom situation.

Sample Plan

Lesson 1

- Brainstorm descriptive words about mice (page 6, Setting the Stage #4).
- Begin KWL Chart (page 9).
- Read *If You Give a Mouse a Cookie.*
- Complete story telling, using pictures as props (page 7, Enjoying the Book #4).
- Create a Roundabout Mousey Story (page 7, #1).
- Conduct A Cheesy Challenge (page 42).

Lesson 2

- Add learned facts to the KWL Chart (page 9).
- Begin poetry and writing activities (pages 23–26).
- Complete Sequencing the Story using story boxes (page 7, #3).
- Make and illustrate a Mousey Accordion Book using story boxes (page 7, #3).
- Create a mouse using the Mousey Math Grid (page 43).

Lesson 3

- Continue with poetry and writing activities (pages 23–26).

- Create Mice Facts Web (page 25).
- Make a personal All About Mice journal entry (page 7, #5).
- Make a Pencil Pal (page 50).
- Have fun with Acrostic Poems (page 8, #6).
- Complete the Cookie Jar Maze (page 16).
- Practice the Mousey Poems and Chants (page 23).

Lesson 4

- Begin a study of Mice Facts (page 44).
- Play the Cat and Mice game (page 8, #9).
- Invent a new kind of mousetrap for saving mice (page 8, #8).
- Continue with poetry and writing activities (pages 23–26). Create a cinquain poem about mice.
- Decorate the poem with Thumbprint Mice (page 50).
- Complete the Telling Time activity (page 32).
- Create Mousey Pet Rocks (page 51).
- Sing some of the Mouse-a-rific Songs (pages 54 and 55).

Overview of Activities

Setting the Stage

1. To obtain factual information about mice you may want to pre-read pages 74–76.

2. To prepare your room for your *Mice* thematic unit, set up the Our Five Senses bulletin board (page 66) and the Mice Learning Center (page 71).

3. Prepare a KWL chart (page 9). Have the children share their thoughts and record what they know and what they want to know about mice. If some of the children's facts are incorrect, still record them on the chart. As the theme progresses, the children can reassess their knowledge and correct the chart. As new facts are discovered, add them to the Learned column.

4. Ask the children to participate in offering descriptive words and phrases pertaining to mice. Record their responses on chart paper. Ask them if they think mice are harmful or helpful, mean or friendly, a pal or a pest. Share that the story you will be reading is about a make-believe, friendly mouse.

Enjoying the Book

1. Lead a discussion about what mice like to eat and where mice like to live. (See pages 74–76 for mice facts.) Show the cover of the book *If You Give a Mouse a Cookie* and ask the children to predict what the events of the story will be.

2. After reading the first page of the story, show the illustration and discuss the main characters. Build excitement about what is going to happen next. From time to time, stop reading and enjoy the illustrations with the children.

3. Discuss what is meant by a circular story. (The definition of a circular story is a story whose pattern continues in such a manner that the beginning of the story is also the end of the story.) Visually demonstrate this by drawing a large circle on chart paper and dividing it into 14 equal "pie" sections. Reread *If You Give a Mouse a Cookie* and draw each of the story events in each section of the wheel. (Draw connector arrows to each section to help the children see the continuous-pattern flow.) Retell the story using the circular-story illustrations.

4. Reproduce on tagboard, color, cut out, and laminate the story props (pages 10 and 11). If desired, enlarge the story props by using the enlarging features of a copying machine. Reread *If You Give a Mouse a Cookie* and use the story props to retell the story, having the children appropriately place the story props sequentially in a pocket chart.

5. Another method for retelling the story is to utilize a felt "story apron." You can make a homemade story apron by cutting out a basic apron shape from a large piece of felt-by-the-yard/meter. Cut small slits in the apron's neck and waist area to create tie holes. Feed a length of ribbon through the holes to make the neck and waist ties. (An alternative is to purchase a pre-made felt apron from Book Props, page 80). Reproduce the story props as directed in #4 above. Attach a small piece of Velcro® to the back of each prop. The Velcro will stick to the felt apron.

Overview of Activities *(cont.)*

Enjoying the Book *(cont.)*

6. Have the children retell the story in their own imaginative way either verbally or with the aid of the story props (pages 10 and 11).

7. Reread *If You Give a Mouse a Cookie.* Have the children add mice facts to the KWL chart (page 9) under the section titled What We Learned. Remind them, when appropriate, that some of the mice facts shared are about make-believe mice.

Extending the Book

1. To help the children become familiar with circular stories (page 6, Enjoying the Book, #3), have them assemble the Roundabout Mousey Story (pages 12 and 13). Cut out the cookie circles as well as the space marked "cut out" on circle A. With circle A on top, hold circles A and B together and push a paper fastener through the center holes; spread fastener prongs. Turn the Roundabout Mousey Story to retell the story. Encourage the children to retell the story with their parents or other family members.

2. Place four or five small objects in small paper bags. (The number of bags needed may vary depending on the number of cooperative groups formed.) Have the children work cooperatively to prepare their own imaginative circular story by choosing one item out of the bag and saying, "If you give a mouse a (item's name), he will want . . . ." Then they pick out the next item and continue using this repetitive pattern until all of the items have been used.

3. Pictorially sequencing the story, using story boxes (pages 14 and 15), allows the children to recall some of the story's main points. The children can work individually or cooperatively. Have the children cut out the boxes and put them in order. Then have them attach the cut boxes to the prepared nine-panel Mousey Accordion Book (page 25). **Note:** The first panel is the title "page," and the remaining eight cut-out panels are for the eight text boxes. Display the assembled accordion books in your room or in the library.

4. Reproduce the Squeaky Mouse pattern (pages 67–69) onto tagboard (one mouse per child). Have the children color, cut out, and assemble their mice using paper fasteners or glue. Display the mice on your Five Senses bulletin-board (page 66).

5. The Mice Facts Web (page 25) is a helpful tool when you have your children brainstorm writing ideas. Follow the directions for making personal journals (page 24). Try to find time to allow your children write daily.

Overview of Activities *(cont.)*

Extending the Book *(cont.)*

---

6. Acrostics are fun and help children develop their imagination and creativity. Working individually, in small cooperative groups, or as a total group, have the children create and illustrate Mice Acrostic Card charts (procedure outlined below.) Display the completed charts in a hallway or on the walls in your room.

   • Provide each child or group of children with five 5" x 7" (13 cm x 18 cm) index cards.

   • Have the children print MICE on the first card and illustrate it. This is the title card.

   • On the remaining four cards, have the children print one letter per card: M-I-C-E along the left-side edge.

   • Have each child or group of children print a sentence or word about mice that includes a word that begins with the letter on their card. If desired, the child/children then draw an illustration about the generated word or sentence. (**Note:** Young children can dictate words or sentences for an older child or adult to print; the children then illustrate the cards.)

7. Have the children use the Mice Facts (pages 44–46) and the Mice Map (page 47) to find where different types of mice live. Discuss with the children what the map represents. When completing the map, they should choose a different color for each species and in the corresponding box. Have them color the corresponding location on the map for each species.

8. Have the children invent a "friendly" save-a-mouse trap. Encourage the children to be imaginative when inventing a trap that does not harm mice. Have them draw their ideas and, if appropriate, label the parts of their inventions. Have the children share how their traps operate.

9. Play the Cat and Mice game. You will need a large play area so that there will be adequate room to run. One child plays the cat. He or she sits in the middle of the play area (as if taking a nap). The rest of the children are the mice. Beside "the cat" are small pieces of cheese (beanbags). When the teacher gives a verbal signal, such as "It's cheese time!" the mice creep up to try to get the cat's cheese. Suddenly, the cat awakens and bellows a loud "meow." This is the signal for the mice to run—or be caught. The cat tries to catch (by tapping them gently on the shoulders) as many mice as possible before they reach their holes (pre-designated safety areas). The caught mice then become cats for the next round. The game is continued in this fashion until eventually all of the mice have been caught. The last mouse caught is the first cat for the next game.

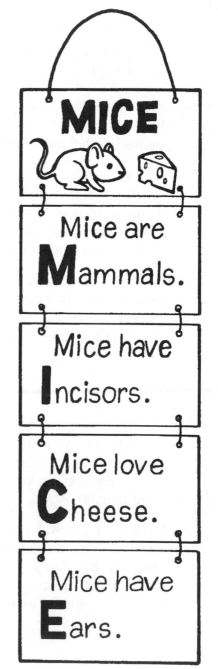

KWL Chart

The KWL chart is a visual aide to help young children classify their thoughts. The chart has three sections: prior knowledge (Know), curiosity knowledge (Want to Know), and acquired knowledge (Learned). Create the chart on paper with the three sections labeled. Have the children tell you what they already know about mice; list their knowledge in the first section. Then have the children tell you what they would like to know about mice; list their ideas in the second section. The last section will be filled in as the unit progresses and the children discover new facts. The chart should be on display during the entire theme. When a Learned fact is discovered that answers a question listed in the Want to Know section, indicate the new information by placing a sticker or a colored star beside the question in the second section as well as adding the learned knowledge to the third section.

KWL charts serve as excellent child-centered resources for providing authentic assessment for evaluation. They can also be a source of information for children as they write stories, illustrate child-created books, and review unit facts.

Know	Want to Know	Learned
Mice have long tails. Mice are not very big. Mice have homes in many places.	Do mice have babies like other furry animals do? What do mice do when it is wintertime? Can mice hear well? How well can mice see?	(This section will be filled in as the unit progresses and facts are discovered.)

A Squeaky Idea: Use three mice as a focal point on your KWL chart. Enlarge the Squeaky Mouse pattern (pages 67–69) three times using an overhead projector or an opaque projector. Cut out and assemble the mice; label and follow the KWL directions as outlined above.

Know

Mice have big ears.

Mice can run fast.

Mice are small.

Want to Know

Do mice live in large families?

Do mice have nests?

Learned

Most mice hunt for food at night.

Mice will eat most foods humans eat.

Story Props

Story Props *(cont.)*

Roundabout Mousey Story

See directions on page 7 for this activity.

If You
Give a Mouse a Cookie,

he will want a . . .

Cut Out

Circle A

12

Roundabout Mousey Story *(cont.)*

Circle B

Story Boxes

The mouse will draw a picture and hang it up.

The mouse will look in the mirror.

The mouse will want a cookie.

The mouse will ask for a glass of milk.

14

Story Boxes *(cont.)*

The mouse will ask for a napkin.

The mouse will sweep every room.

The mouse will need some tape.

The mouse will want to take a nap.

Cookie Jar Maze

Help the mouse find the correct path to the cookie.

16

Town Mouse Country Mouse

By Jan Brett

Summary

Town Mouse Country Mouse *is a famous fable about two mice living in two very different environments. The Town Mouse and the Country Mouse both thought that if they changed their homes and their surroundings their lives would be safer and more relaxing. When they traded lifestyles, though, they discovered new perils and dangers. Eventually they agreed, "There's no place like home."*

The outline below is a suggested plan for using the various activities presented in this unit. You can adapt these ideas to fit your own classroom situation.

Sample Plan

Lesson 1

- Sing Mouse-a-rific Songs (pages 54 and 55).

- Read *Town Mouse Country Mouse*.

- Make Mouse Cookies and Mint Tea (page 56).

- Complete the Who Was It? activity (page 22).

- Compare and contrast the Town Mouse and the Country Mouse (page 18, Enjoying the Book, #2).

- Work on daily poetry and writing activities (pages 23–26).

- Create a new mouse house (page 19, #3).

- Play a mousey Simon Says (page 19, #4).

Lesson 2

- Read another version of the Country Mouse and the City Mouse (pages 20 and 21). Compare this version to Jan Brett's version using a Venn diagram.

- Create a Mousey Mini-book (page 26).

- Make mousey stick puppets. Use stick puppets to retell story (page 19, #5).

- Continue with the poetry and writing activities (pages 23–26).

- Learn some healthy, nutritional eating facts (page 19, #6).

Lesson 3

- Complete the Mousey Word Search (page 27).

- Review the Mousey Poems and Chants (page 23) and Mouse-a-rific Songs (pages 54 and 55).

- Read and compare two mouse fables (pages 28–30).

- Explore a mouse's sense of taste and smell (page 19, #7).

- Complete the Country Mouse activity (pages 48 and 49).

Lesson 4

- Continue studying the senses by examining sight, touch, and hearing (pages 37–39).

- Introduce the Parts of a Letter (page 31).

- Practice writing a letter to Town Mouse or Country Mouse (page 19, #11).

- Plan your culminating activities (page 19, #12).

- Prepare and send invitations (page 73).

Overview of Activities

Setting the Stage

1. Reproduce the Mouse-a-rific Songs (pages 54 and 55) onto chart paper. Begin each morning with a song to set the mood for the day.

2. Create a burrow entrance by decorating your doorway. To create a tunnel-like look, cover the door itself with black bulletin-board paper. Create an "arch" of brown bulletin-board paper that covers the sides and top of the doorframe and a portion of the wall itself. Add paper rocks near the base of the left and right sides of the burrow entrance. On the covered door area, using white, cutout letters, add the title: Mouse-rific Learning! Enter Here!"

3. Create the Our Five Senses bulletin board (page 66), if you have not already done so.

4. Lead a discussion or review about where mice live and what mice like to eat. Discuss what dangers a town mouse would encounter in the country and a country mouse would encounter in the city. From this discussion, lead into reading the story. Show the cover of *Town Mouse Country Mouse*. Ask the children to predict what the events of the story will be.

Enjoying the Book

1. When the story is completed, lead a discussion of the story's events. Talk about the dangers each mouse encountered and how these dangers could have been avoided if they had been content to stay in their own environments.

2. Compare the lives of the two mice. Have the children focus on their similarities and differences. (This activity can be done using a Venn Diagram.) As a follow up, conduct a survey to find out if your children would rather be town mice or country mice.

3. Learn more about real mice by completing the Mousey Word Search (page 27) as a total group. Provide each child with a copy of page 27 or make an overhead transparency of this activity to use as a total group on an overhead projector. As the children search for each word, define or have them define the word. Encourage them to use the word in a sentence. After all the words have been found, have them try to solve the riddle at the bottom of the page. The answer to the riddle is *catnap*.

Extending the Book

1. There are many Town Mouse and Country Mouse story versions. Read some of them (Bibliography, page 79). A fable version can also be found on pages 20 and 21. If possible, record the fable on a cassette tape and place it in a listening center. After the children listen to the recorded fable, have them illustrate their favorite part. Decorate the listening area with their illustrations.

Overview of Activities *(cont.)*

2. Recite daily some of the Mousey Poems and Chants (page 23) and the Mouse-a-rific Songs (pages 54 and 55) for enjoyment and vocabulary development.

3. In large or small groups, create mouse houses. An imaginary mouse house might be a shoe, teapot, box, pumpkin, log, etc. Using 12" x 18" (30 cm x 46 cm) sheets of construction paper, have the children draw their new mouse houses; display.

4. Turn the popular children's game "Simon Says" into a "Country (Town) Mouse Says" game. This game can be played indoors or outdoors.

5. Prepare the stick puppets (pages 52 and 53). Then, using the puppets, act out *The Country Mouse and The City Mouse* fable (pages 20 and 21). To prepare the stick puppets, see page 51.

6. Classify foods commonly eaten by mice. Reproduce the Mousey Food Pyramid (page 33), two per child. Have them fill in the first chart with the common foods mice eat (nuts, berries, cheese, seeds, vegetables, etc.) by drawing small illustrations. Discuss the importance of eating a balanced diet. Then fill in the second chart based on the food-group guidelines indicated for human consumption by illustrating the suggested serving amounts. Compare the two pyramids to see if mice eat "balanced" meals, similar to what people should eat. Finish this activity by making and eating Mouse Salads (page 56).

7. Prepare for studying the five senses by following the directions on page 34. Then reread the story and use the appropriate sense questions, also found on page 34.

8. Complete the smell and taste activities (pages 35–37). Refer back to the story's text and illustrations to discover where the mice used their senses of smell and taste.

9. Complete the senses activities for seeing and hearing (pages 37 and 38). As a follow-up activity, take a walk around your school, nearby park, or woods to listen for sounds and observe the sights. Upon returning to the classroom, divide the children into four groups. Each group will create a senses chart. Hand out a piece of chart paper to each group and have the children illustrate one thing they saw and one thing they heard on the walk. Have each group share their illustrations.

10. To enjoy the sense of touch, ask the children to bring in a soft toy from home. Have the children share their toys during a show-and-tell time. Place the children into pairs, or small groups, and allow them to play with each other's soft toys.

11. Practice the parts of a letter by completing the activity found on page 31. Then have the children choose which mouse they would like to be, the Town Mouse or the Country Mouse. Have them write a letter to the other mouse, emphasizing the need to follow the sequential parts of a letter. Have the children decorate their letters to reflect who wrote it (the Town Mouse or the Country Mouse). Have the children read their letters orally; display the finished products.

12. Plan a mouse-a-rific party. Send invitations (page 73) to parents, administration, or other classes. Practice the Mouse-a-rific Songs (pages 54 and 55) and Mouse Poems and Chants (page 23), as well as prepare to present the *Belling the Cat* Choral Play (pages 64 and 65). You may want to include tasty snacks to "nibble" on during the party, plus pass out awards (page 72) as take-home mementos.

Country Mouse and City Mouse

Once upon a time, Country Mouse asked City Mouse to come for a visit.

When City Mouse arrived, the two mice sat down to a delicious dinner of corn and seedcakes. City Mouse ate just a little, but Country Mouse ate up everything.

"Don't you like my corn and seedcakes?" asked Country Mouse.

"Not really," said City Mouse. "I like city food. You must come to my house and try some."

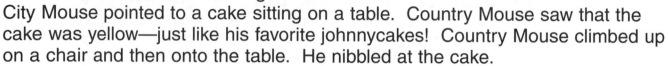

Early the next morning, Country Mouse set off for the city with City Mouse. City Mouse took his friend into a big room. City Mouse pointed to a cake sitting on a table. Country Mouse saw that the cake was yellow—just like his favorite johnnycakes! Country Mouse climbed up on a chair and then onto the table. He nibbled at the cake.

"S-h-h!" said City Mouse. "I hear the Tall One coming. Hurry. Run towards my mouse house."

A door opened and a lady came into the room. Country Mouse scurried off the table and ran for the small hole in the corner as fast as he could. The mice watched as the Tall One put the cake away. Then she left the room. Country Mouse was shaking.

"Don't be afraid," said City Mouse. "She can't catch us. We can run fast."

"Can-n-n we go back and find something else good to eat?" whispered Country Mouse.

"Look up high. Can you see the open cupboard door?" asked City Mouse. "Let's go see what's in there."

City Mouse and Country Mouse sneaked out of the hole and up to the open cupboard door. "M-m-m-m!" said City Mouse. "Look, a bag of sweet candy."

Country Mouse started to nibble on the candy. "How tasty! What fun this is. I wish that I had candy like this to eat all the time."

Country Mouse and City Mouse *(cont.)*

Just then, the kitchen door creaked open slowly. "M-e-o-w."

"Run, Country Mouse, run!" shouted City Mouse. Country Mouse dropped his sweet treat and ran as fast as he could. When they were safely back in the mouse-house hole, City Mouse said, "That was Cat. He likes to eat mice, but he's not very good at catching me."

Country Mouse told City Mouse that he wanted to go back to his country home where he felt safe. He didn't like feeling scared.

"Wait," said City Mouse, "I'll take you to the Tall One's basement. It is safe and she has good things to nibble on in there, too."

They crawled down the long stairway to the basement. Country Mouse saw baskets filled with grains and nuts. He ran around nibbling all the tasty treats. Then he saw something big and yellow. It looked so-o-o good!

"I must try some of that yellow candy," he told City Mouse, putting out his paw.

City Mouse looked up. "No, Country Mouse! Stop!" he yelled. "That's a mousetrap!"

"What's a mousetrap?" asked Country Mouse.

"A mousetrap is not our friend. It can catch you and hurt you," said City Mouse.

"I do not like it here! I do not like traps. I do not like the Tall One, and I do not like Cat! I am going home to my country house."

> **Moral: Be thankful for what you have—not what others seem to have.**

Who Was It?

Read the sentences. Put a Town Mouse or Country Mouse in each box.

Went for a visit to the country.	**Ate sweets and crumbs on the table.**	**Was frightened by a mousetrap.**
Was caught by the tail.	**Was afraid of the rain.**	**Lived in a fine house with many rooms.**
Loved the smell of cheese.	**Loved the moon and sunrise.**	**Liked the hustle and bustle.**

Cut and paste.

22

Mousey Poems and Chants

Poems composed by Michele McBride

My Friend, the Mouse

There is a little furry mouse,
Who likes to come inside my house.
He does not use the big front door,
He pops up through a hole in the floor.
At first he gave me quite a scare,
His wee, black eyes and light-gray hair.
He looked so tiny and so sweet,
With a wiggly nose and tiny feet.
But when I got a closer peek,
He did not make me want to shriek.
His face was very kind,
A new little friend I did find!

Mice I Know

I know a little mouse named Bill,
Who sits upon my windowsill.
He has a friend whose name is Elf
Who likes to sit upon my shelf.
Elf has a friend whose name is Bert
Who loves to hide inside my shirt.
Bert has a friend whose name is Sue,
Who plays hide-and-seek inside my shoe.
Sue has a friend whose name is Mike,
Who rides in the basket of my bike.
Mike has a friend whose name is Tess,
Who wears a pretty flowered dress.
I really do know a lot of mice,
And all of them are very nice!

What Do Mice Do?

What does a mouse do everyday?
Does he work, or does he play?
Does he sing, or does he dance?
Does he clean his shirt and pants?
Does he watch a TV show?
Does he have his lawn to mow?
Does he talk on the telephone?
Does he munch an ice-cream cone?
Does he go and learn at school?
Or have a dip in the swimming pool?
No—mice don't live this way at all,
They don't go shopping or catch a ball.
They look for food and sleep a bit,
Or walk around, or maybe sit.
They might hide in your shoes or hat,
Or run away from a big, mean cat!

Mice

Mice skitter and squeak as they play,
They search for food all day.
Then hurry home to cozy beds,
To rest their tired and weary heads.
When dawn appears once more,
Off they scamper under the door.

Writing Experiences

Squeaky Mouse Poems

With your children, brainstorm a chart listing descriptive mouse words, noises, or actions mice make, and what feelings mice might have. Then have the children write their own poems or chants.
Note: Brainstormed words can also be used for creative-writing experiences.

Mousey Size		Mousey Noises/Actions		Mousey Feelings	
tiny	wee	creeping	scampering	nervous	scared
little	teeny	skittering	dancing	shy	bold
small	miniature	gnawing	nibbling	proud	spry
		squeaking	chewing	sly	coy

Cinquain Poem

A cinquain is a poem that consists of five specific lines.

Line 1 – One noun

Line 2 – Two describing words for mice

Line 3 – Three words that describe actions of mice

Line 4 – Four words that express feelings mice might show

Line 5 – One word that refers to the title (different word)

Mice
Tiny, Furry
Squeaking, Skittering, Gnawing
They are very shy
Gray

Personal Journals

Encouraging your children to keep a personal journal helps them to express themselves through both written and oral language. Allow time for both writing and sharing their stories with one another.

Keep in mind that these journals are personal. When you read a child's journal, it is to understand that child's thought, not to focus on perfect penmanship or skill ability. Respond verbally or by writing a note of encouragement.

Journal-writing topics may be open-ended or include such topics as facts learned; personal feelings about, or experiences with, mice; summaries of activities completed during the mice unit; and imaginative stories about mice.

Personal journals can also serve as an excellent child-centered authentic assessment that assists you in evaluating whether the language skills you have introduced are becoming personal strategies.

Writing Experiences *(cont.)*

Mice Facts Web

A semantic thought web is a graphic organizer that can help children categorize information. The mice web can be completed individually, in a small group, or as a whole-class activity.

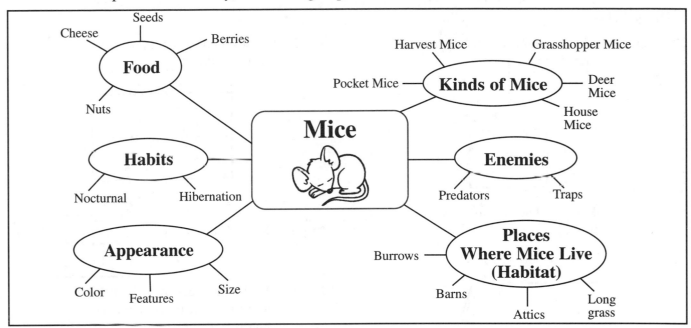

Mousey Accordion Book

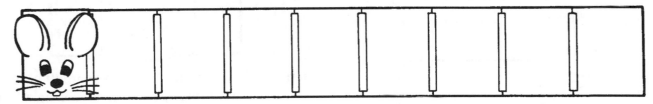

Materials

- nine 8½" x 11" (22 cm x 28 cm) pieces of tagboard
- pink, gray, and black construction-paper scraps
- pencil
- scissors
- transparent tape
- glue

Directions

1. Lay the nine pieces of tagboard face down on a flat surface.

2. Tape the pieces together on the "seam lines."

3. Cut out the story mini-pages (pages 14 and 15) and glue one mini-page per panel (starting with the second panel from the left). Have the children illustrate the pages.

4. On the remaining panel, add free-hand drawn ears, eyes, nose, and mouth using the pencil and scraps of gray, pink, and black construction paper.

5. Display the accordion-style book for all to see and read.

Mousey Mini-book

Materials

- one sheet of 12" x 18" (30 cm x 46 cm) white construction paper (per child)
- scissors

Directions

Step 1   Fold the construction paper in half.

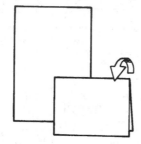

Step 2   Fold the construction paper in half again.

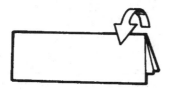

Step 3   Fold the paper in half sideways; reopen.

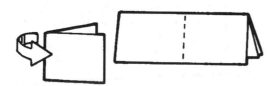

Step 4   Reopen again by lifting the folded edge upward (the paper will appear to have four squares). Cut halfway through the folded edge.

Step 5   Completely open up the paper and turn it sideways.

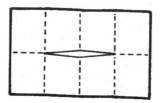

Step 6   Refold the paper.

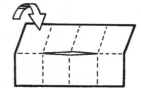

Step 7   Push the ends towards the center and the mini-book pages will begin to fall into place.

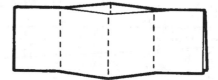

Step 8   Fold over the "page" in your left hand towards the pages held in your right hand; crease the pages to form the mini-book.

Step 9   *Optional:* Glue the "open centers" of each page to form succinct pages.

26

Mousey Word Search

E	N	E	M	I	E	S	C	L	A	W	S
S	E	E	D	S	O	W	L	S	O	N	R
C	H	E	E	S	E	H	A	W	K	O	F
S	W	A	N	G	E	A	M	R	S	C	R
H	T	H	M	C	A	T	M	A	Q	T	U
G	R	A	I	N	S	P	A	K	U	U	I
N	A	M	I	S	C	A	M	P	E	R	T
H	P	O	N	L	K	S	E	K	A	N	S
O	N	I	B	B	L	E	P	O	K	A	E
L	R	O	T	I	R	R	R	R	E	T	L	N
E	I	N	C	I	S	O	R	S	V	N	K
M	S	N	O	U	T	R	O	D	E	N	T

Word Bank

cat	gnaws	mammal	owls	snout
cheese	grains	mice	rodent	squeak
claws	hawk	nest	scamper	tail
enemies	hole	nibble	seeds	trap
fruits	incisors	nocturnal	snakes	whiskers

Unscramble the **shaded square letters** to solve the riddle.

What do cats to do after chasing mice? _____

Comparing Mouse Fables

Traditionally, a fable is a short, make-believe story that teaches a moral. In most fables the main character is an animal that talks and acts like a human being. A moral or lesson is summed up at the end in the form of a proverb. Two of Aesop's fables, *The Lion and the Mouse* and *The Cat and the Mice*, are found on pages 29 and 30. Read, or have your children read, the two fables. Then use a Venn diagram to compare the two fables.

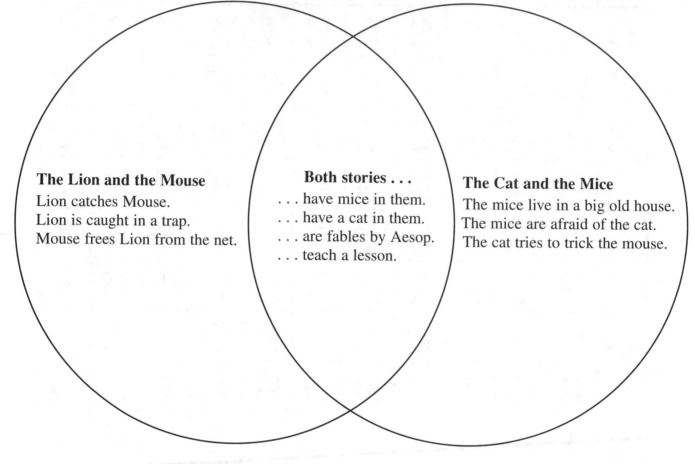

The Lion and the Mouse
Lion catches Mouse.
Lion is caught in a trap.
Mouse frees Lion from the net.

Both stories . . .
. . . have mice in them.
. . . have a cat in them.
. . . are fables by Aesop.
. . . teach a lesson.

The Cat and the Mice
The mice live in a big old house.
The mice are afraid of the cat.
The cat tries to trick the mouse.

Studying Mouse Fables

Well-written stories have a beginning, middle, and an ending. Pass out a jumbo-size sheet of construction paper (one per child). Have each child turn the paper vertically, fold it in thirds, and label each section respectively with the words *beginning*, *middle*, and *ending*. (An adult can also do this step.) Ask the children to illustrate a beginning, middle, and ending portion of one of the shared fables and illustrate each section of their construction paper respectively. Encourage children to write sentences to complement the illustrations.

Note: This activity can also be done in cooperative groups of three. Have each group member illustrate one of the three elements.

Beginning
_____
Middle
_____
Ending
_____

The Lion and the Mouse

One day Lion was asleep in his den. Mouse, not watching where he was running, ran into Lion's den and over Lion's nose. Lion awoke with a roar and grabbed Mouse with his huge paw.

He opened his jaws. "M-m-m-m. I am going to eat you for lunch."

"No!" cried Mouse. "Please don't eat me. Please let me go. If you let me go, I will never forget your kindness. Then someday I will help you."

Lion smiled at Mouse. Even though Lion knew Mouse could never help him, he opened his paw and let Mouse go.

One day, a long time after Lion had let Mouse go, Lion was out looking for food. He did not watch where he was going and fell into a net trap. He clawed and kicked at the heavy ropes, but he could not get himself out of the trap.

He roared, "I will never get out of here!" All the leaves shook on the trees.

Mouse heard Lion and went running to look for him. When he saw Lion, he said, "Here I am, Mr. Lion. I can help you."

Lion roared again. "What can a little mouse like you do to help me?" he asked.

"You will see," said Mouse. "You helped me. Now I will help you."

Mouse began to work. He nibbled at the net's ropes with his sharp teeth. He worked and worked and worked until he had cut a big hole in the net.

Lion jumped out of the trap. "Thank you, Mouse," he said. "You may be a little mouse, but you just got me out of a big trap. We will be friends forever."

Moral: Do for others what you would want them to do for you.

The Cat and the Mice

There once was an old house that was overrun with mice. The mice enjoyed their life in the old house because no one bothered them.

One day Cat walked by this old house and said to herself, "That's just the right place for me to live!" So she moved in and curled up on an old rug.

Soon she became hungry and looked around for food. She discovered her favorite kind—mice. She began to catch them one by one.

The mice became very afraid of Cat. They stayed in their hole-house in the walls of the house.

"Meow! This is not fair!" meowed Cat, "Come out, mice. I'm hungry!"

"I know what I'll do," Cat thought to herself. "I'll lie down on my rug and pretend to be dead. Then they will come out to see what has happened to me—and I'll catch them."

Cat lay still. Soon a scout mouse peeked its head out of its hole and spied Cat.

"Squeak, squeak!" cried scout mouse. "You might think you are clever, Cat, but you can't trick me. You are not dead. I can see you breathing."

Cat now realized that the mice were clever and would not be easily tricked. She decided the best thing to do was to move on to another old house. The mice danced with joy when Cat left—forever.

Moral: Don't trust anyone who tries to trick you.

Parts of a Letter

To encourage your children to remember the parts of a letter, teach them with this fun, bodily-kinesthetic activity.

Reproduce the chart (at right) and enlarge it to poster size. Color, cut out, and hang it at eye level where all your children can easily see it. Stand next to the poster, with your feet slightly wider than shoulder-width apart. State the following facts (*as well as make the movement indicated in the italic parentheses*).

The parts of a letter are divided into three sections. The Heading (*move your index finger in a rotating fashion clock-wise around your head*) is the first part of a letter. It includes the Date (*point to your eyes and dramatically look towards the classroom calendar*), which we get from the calendar, and the Opening (*as you state this word, place your index finger just inside your mouth and bring it forward as you say . . .*) ". . . Dear Jane, . . . Dear John . . . Dear Aunt Sally . . ."

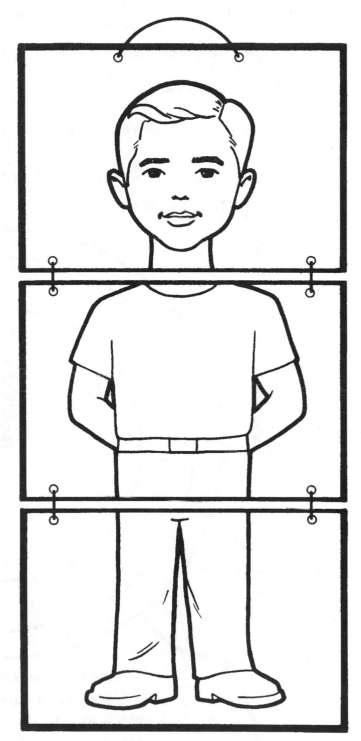

The next part of a letter is the Body (*take one hand and place it horizontally at your neck; place your other hand horizontally near your mid-thigh area*). The body of a letter is where you write what you want to say. It is the longest part of a letter.

The last part of a letter is called the Closing (*simultaneously jump up and bring your feet together, symbolizing a "closing" motion*). The closing tells the reader that you are done writing. Pretend that I am standing in a mud puddle. If I jump up and land with my feet closed and then move out of the mud, what will still be in the mud puddle? (Allow your children to respond.) That's right, my footprints—-and that's my signature (*pretend like you are stepping out of the mud puddle and point to your [invisible] footprints*).

After your children have had a few chances to kinesthetically try the movements, have them draw a picture of themselves and label their illustrations with the parts-of-a-letter terminology.

Telling Time

Using the word bank, write the time words around the clock starting with number 1.

1. Fall is one s __ __ __ __ __ of the year.

2. You eat lunch at 12:00 __ __ __ n.

3. The opposite of day is __ __ __ __ t.

4. A part of a school year is called a t __ __ __ .

5. An hour has sixty m __ __ __ __ __ s.

6. One minute has sixty __ __ __ __ __ __ s.

Word Box

night
term
minutes
season
seconds
noon

Hickory, dickory, dock
The mouse ran up the clock.
The clock struck one,
The mouse ran down,
Hickory, dickory, dock.

Mousey Food Pyramid

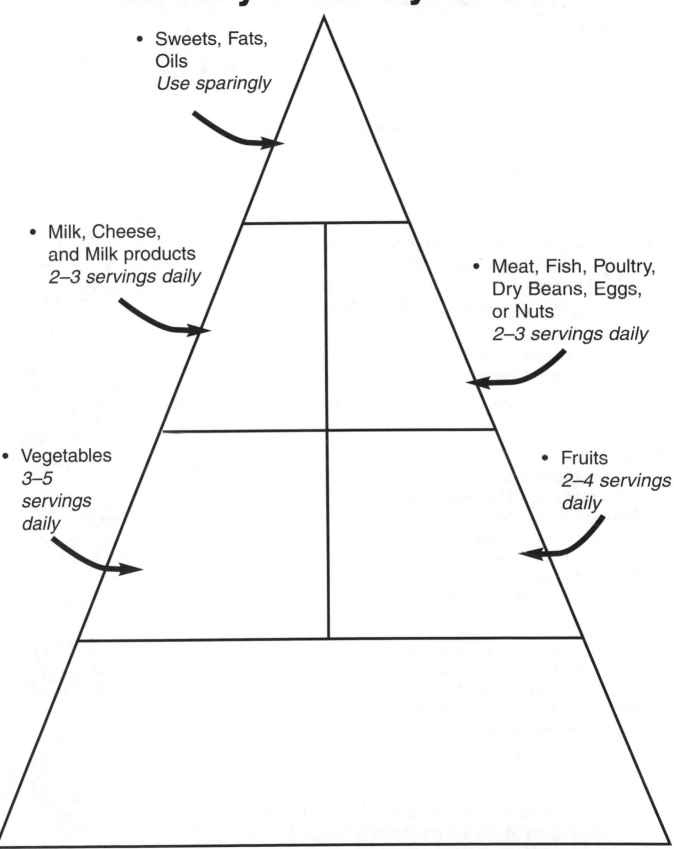

- Sweets, Fats, Oils
Use sparingly

- Milk, Cheese, and Milk products
2–3 servings daily

- Meat, Fish, Poultry, Dry Beans, Eggs, or Nuts
2–3 servings daily

- Vegetables
3–5 servings daily

- Fruits
2–4 servings daily

Breads, Cereals, Rice, and Pasta   *6–11 servings daily*

Studying Mouse Senses

Preparation

Display five reproduced and cutout mice faces (pattern, page 67) on a bulletin board. Label each face using a cutout paper arrow pointing to each focused sense. **Note:** For feel, add a reproduced and cutout mouse arm and hand (page 69).

Sense Questions

Use these questions, based on Jan Brett's *Town Mouse Country Mouse*, for the smell and taste activities found on pages 35–37.

Smell

- What did Country Mouse smell in the house early in the morning?
- What did Town Mouse smell in the meadow?
- What did Country Mouse smell coming from the box on the shelf?
- What smells seemed wonderful to Town Mouse?

Smell

Taste

- What did Country Mouse stuff in her mouth?
- What did Town Mouse want to taste?

Taste

Use these question with the see and hear activities found on pages 37 and 38 and 40 and 41.

See

- What did Town Mouse see on his picnic in the country?
- What did Country Mouse see up on the shelf?
- What did the blackbird see?
- What did Country Mouse see out of the window?
- What did Town Mouse see after the rain stopped?
- What did Country Mouse see on a pine board?
- What did Town Mouse see from the tree?

See

Hear

- What did Country Mouse hear Town Mouse exclaim?
- What did Country Mouse hear the next morning?
- What noise scared Town Mouse as he was thrown across the room?
- What did Town Mouse hear in the underbrush?
- What sound seemed cheerful and friendly when Town Mouse got home?

Hear

Use these questions with the feel versus feelings activities found on page 39.

Touch/Feel

- How did Town Mouse feel when he woke up after his dream?
- How did Country Mouse feel after he had searched for food?
- How did Town Mouse feel when he saw the countryside?
- How did Town Mouse feel when he was out looking for blackberries?

Touch

Studying Mouse Senses *(cont.)*

Smell and Taste

Materials

- Jan Brett's version of *Town Mouse Country Mouse* (page 17)
- five mice faces (Preparation, page 34)
- 3" x 5" (8 cm x 13 cm) index cards
- permanent black marker
- chart paper
- magazines
- scissors
- tape
- peanut butter in a sealed jar labeled "mystery jar"
- spreading knife
- crackers

Directions

1. Begin the lesson by showing the children the five mice senses illustrations. Remind them that we use our nose to smell and our tongue to taste. Tell them that mice have a strong sense of smell and taste. They can smell food from a distance far away. Explain that mice, just like people, use their senses to help discover what is in the world around them.

2. Revisit the illustrations in *Town Mouse Country Mouse.* Try to identify things that the mice smelled and tasted. List the brainstormed ideas on the index cards using the marker and place completed cards underneath the posted Smell and Taste mice faces.

3. Using the chart paper, create two charts: Things We Smell; Things We Taste. Using old magazines, have the children cut out appropriate pictures and tape them onto the respective charts. Some things may suit both charts so the children will have to decide where they would like to place those items.

4. Ask the children the question, "Do you think you can smell as well as a mouse?" Show the children the sealed "mystery jar." Have the children pretend they are mice and stand at the back of a (typical-size) classroom. Remove the lid of the jar and ask the children to take a deep breath and try to smell what's in the jar. Explain that a mouse would be able to smell from that distance. Ask the children to move two steps closer and take another deep breath. Can they smell what is in the jar now? Continue this process until someone can finally smell and identify the peanut butter.

5. When a mouse smells something as a good as peanut butter, it definitely wants to taste it! As a conclusion to this lesson, spread a small amount of peanut butter onto the crackers and have the children "sniff" their peanut-butter treat before tasting it. The children will have learned from this experience that people cannot smell as well as mice.

Science

Studying Mouse Senses *(cont.)*

Smell and Taste Game

Materials

- four separate trays of fruit, (such as apples, oranges, lemons, and grapes) cut into bite-size pieces
- a paper plate
- a blindfold
- paper towels

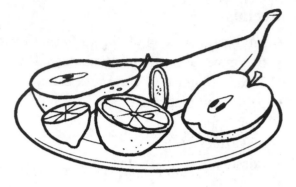

Directions

1. Place a sample of four different fruit pieces on a plate.

2. Loosely blindfold one child at a time and ask him or her to smell each cut-fruit sample.

3. Have the child try to identify the types of fruit. When the child has identified the fruits, remove the pieces from the plate and place them on a paper towel for the child to eat.

A Smelling Activity

Materials

- baby-food jars or paper cups
- samples of coffee granules, tea leaves, cinnamon oil, crushed cloves, garlic salt, chili powder, soap powder, or other pungent-smelling items
- cotton balls
- flower pattern (below)
- colored construction paper
- scissors

Preparations

1. Place one smelling sample (such as cinnamon oil) on a cotton ball and place the ball inside a baby food jar or paper cup; set aside. Label the smelling jar/cup by writing an identifying symbol on the bottom of the jar or cup. Repeat the process for the remaining to-be-smelled items.

2. Using construction paper, reproduce and cut out flowers and flower centers using the provided pattern or draw free hand. Place one flower shape on the top of each jar or cup.

Studying Mouse Senses *(cont.)*

A Smelling Activity *(cont.)*

Directions

1. Explain or review that we use our nose to smell and our tongue to taste. Have the children point to their noses and take a deep breath.

2. Invite the children, one at a time, to smell each flower cup using his or her nose and a deep breath. (Ask the children to place their hands behind their back so they will not be tempted to use them.) Ask the children to tell you what they think they smelled. List responses on chart paper, if desired.

3. After all the children have had a turn smelling the flower cups, reveal what the smells represent.

Seeing and Hearing Game

Materials

- See and Hear Cards (page 40)
- My Eyes, My Ears sheet (page 41)
- scissors
- crayons
- a cassette tape of sounds
- 10 or more objects, arranged on a tray
- towel
- chart paper

Preparations

1. Reproduce the See and Hear Cards onto tagboard. Cut apart the cards, color, and laminate them for durability. You will need to reproduce enough cards so that every child receives a card.

2. Reproduce the My Eyes, My Ears sheet, one per child.

Directions

1. Pass out one See or one Hear card to each child, face down. Explain that the game is played by having them move around the room trying to find classmates with the same type (see or hear) of card. Before they begin, be certain you explain that the children with Hear cards (animals or things) can make sounds or noises, but the children with See cards cannot make sounds, instead they must pantomime their pictured item.

Studying Mouse Senses *(cont.)*

Seeing and Hearing Game *(cont.)*

2. Tell the children the signal to begin the game will be a seeing signal (dropping a piece of paper on a desk). The signal to end the game will be a hearing signal (clapping your hands). Begin by dropping the paper. Hearing-card children will begin to make their appropriate sounds while the Seeing-card children will begin their pantomimes.

3. After about three to four minutes, clap your hands and have each group display their cards. As a total class, decide if the groups have classified themselves (seeing or hearing) correctly. Permit children input in this evaluation.

4. Have the children complete the My Eyes, My Ears activity sheet. Be certain your children understand the concepts of *up* versus *down*, and *loud* versus *soft*, before completing this activity.

Note: As an extension, record familiar sounds (coughing, snoring, sneezing, telephone ringing, radio playing, car horn honking, etc.) onto a cassette tape. Play the tape and have the children try to recognize the sounds. Replay the tape and discuss each sound.

An extension activity for See would be to arrange objects familiar to the children on a tray. Have the children look carefully at each item in order to remember as many items as they can. Cover the tray with a towel and ask them to recall as many items as they can. Remove the towel and discuss which items were remembered and which were forgotten, if any.

Listening-in Game

Directions

1. Divide the class into groups of three or four children. Have each group go to a different area within the classroom or on the playground.

2. Have the groups listen for two minutes and record all of the sounds they hear, such as water running, voices, birds, wind, bells, ticking clock, etc.

3. After the time is up, call all of the groups together. Have each group share the sounds that they heard.

4. Compare the lists to see if the sounds were the same or different, depending on where the group was while listening for their sounds.

Another variation to this game is for a child to hide behind a desk or screen (so he or she cannot be seen) and make a sound, such as breaking sticks or tearing paper. The class then tries to guess what the sound is.

38

Studying Mouse Senses *(cont.)*

Feel Versus Feelings

Materials

- samples of textured fabric (wool, cotton, velvet, terry cloth, burlap, silk, etc.)
- samples of toys (soft, smooth, heavy, and light)
- samples of indoor and outdoor objects (such as wool, macaroni, walnut shells, marbles, feathers, leaves, etc.)
- chart paper
- paper bags
- pictures from magazines or books that show people's emotions (happy, sad, scared, loving, etc.)
- 3" x 5" (8 cm x 13 cm) index cards

Directions

1. Begin by asking the children to feel the samples of fabrics and share how they feel when they touch them. List the descriptive words the children express on chart paper.

2. Display a variety of toys. Allow some of the children to choose a toy to describe how the toy literally feels. Encourage expressive descriptive words; add the words to the chart.

   (**Note:** For fun, have the children use descriptive words based on feeling the items with their toes, faces, or arms.)

3. Explain to the children that when we describe how things feel (by touching them), we can also express our feelings (our emotions). Introduce the concept of emotions. Show pictures wherein people are showing various emotions. Ask the children to describe the emotions in each picture. Have the children share times they have felt scared, angry, happy, etc.

4. Place objects (wool, macaroni, walnut shells, marbles, feathers, leaves, etc.) separately into the paper bags. Have the children feel the items inside the bags. Encourage them to express their emotional feelings about their reactions to physically feeling the items. (**Note:** The bag containing the macaroni may contain cooked macaroni to incite instant emotional feelings!) Reinforce that sometimes when we feel with our skin it makes us have a certain emotional feeling.

To conclude the lesson, review the story *Town Mouse Country Mouse* to see if there were any times that the mice literally felt something by touching it that caused them to express a special emotional feeling. For example, when Country Mouse landed on the soft fur of the sleeping cat he had a scared feeling. When an enormous black bird carried off Town Mouse he felt frightened. Write some of the tactile- and emotional-feeling descriptive words generated onto the chart paper onto index cards and place them under the Touch and Feel mice faces respectively (Preparation page 34).

See and Hear Cards

See   **Hear**

My Eyes, My Ears

Does it sound loud or soft? Mark the box. Color the pictures.

Hear	Loud	Soft

Would you look up or down? Mark the box. Color the pictures.

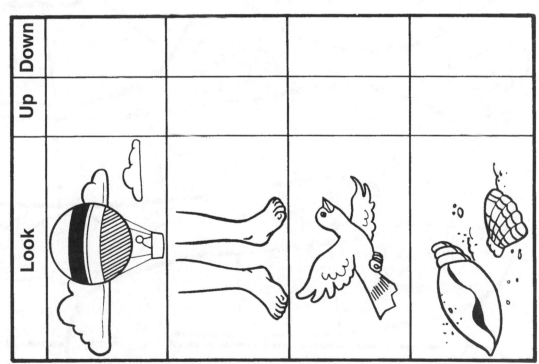

Look	Up	Down

A Cheesy Challenge

Can you reach the cheese? Roll a die and follow the path. You must roll the exact number on the die to finally get the cheese!

Start

Name a kind of mouse and move ahead 2 spaces.

Take the shortcut!

You spot a trap! Jump ahead 2 spaces.

You stop to chase a bird. Miss a turn.

Mice run fast. Go ahead 2 spaces.

You stop to look in the pond. Miss a turn.

You found a book to read. Take another turn.

You rest under the toadstools. Miss a turn.

Take a shortcut.

You stop to play with a mouse friend. Miss a turn.

If you can say a word that rhymes with mouse, go ahead 2 spaces.

Mr. Tom scares you. Jump ahead 2 spaces.

Mousey Math Grid

Use the grid pattern in the top box to draw the mouse in the bottom box.

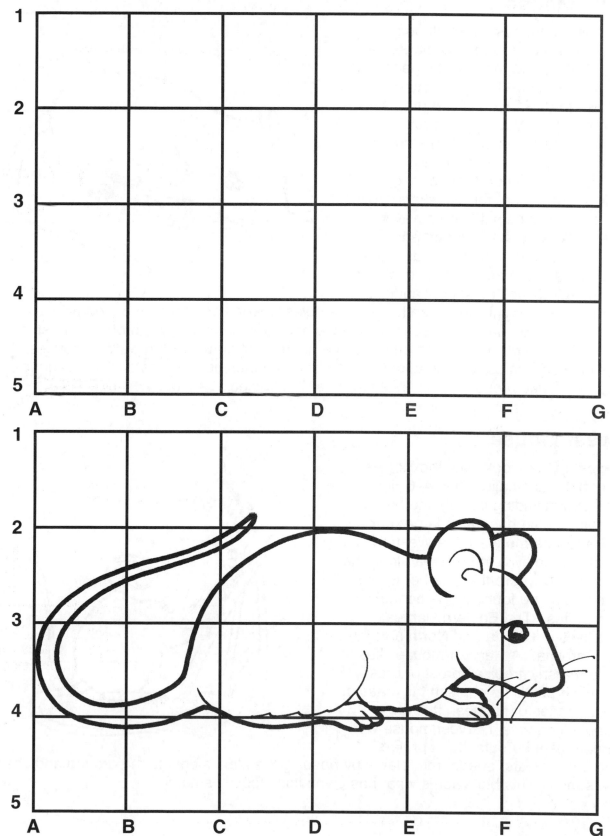

Mice Facts

House Mouse

The House mouse is the most common mouse. It can be found in Canada, the United States, and Mexico. Its head and body measure 2½–3½" (6.5–9 cm) long, and it weighs ½–1 oz. (14–28 grams). It has brownish-gray fur on its back and lighter gray fur on its side and stomach. Its tail is longer than its body and has no fur. It has a small head and a long, narrow snout. Long, thin whiskers grow from its snout to help it find its way in the dark. Its ears are rounded and its eyes look like small, round beads. The House mouse eats anything that humans eat, as well as soap, candles,

and glue. With its chisel-like teeth, it gnaws holes in wood and tears into food packages. This unwanted "house guest" has a strong, flexible body and can squeeze through very small openings. It can climb well and can often be heard running within the walls of houses. Its nest is located in a dark place and is lined with soft materials, such as clothing or upholstery scraps. A House mouse usually has four to seven babies at a time.

Harvest Mouse

A Harvest mouse looks like the House mouse, but it is smaller. It is 4–6" long (10–15 cm) including its tail, and has hair on its tail. It also has much larger ears than the House mouse. The Western Harvest mouse lives in the area along the Pacific Ocean where the weather is warm, but it can also be found in the central United States. The Eastern Harvest mouse lives in Florida and North and South Carolina. A Harvest mouse likes to live in a marshy, tropical forest or grassy meadow. It builds its nests in tall grass or in the branches of bushes. It is an excellent climber. A Harvest mouse will eat green plant sprouts, but it prefers

seeds. It "harvests" seeds from plants by bending the plant stems to the ground and chewing off the seeds. This behavior is what has given this mouse its name.

Mice Facts *(cont.)*

Grasshopper Mouse

The Grasshopper mouse lives in the prairies of Canada and the United States. It is about the same size as the House mouse, but it looks fatter. It has a thick, short, white-tipped tail. Its body fur is brown or gray. Unlike most other mice, the Grasshopper mouse prefers to eat meat rather than plants. It likes to feed on grasshoppers, but also enjoys eating beetles, crickets, caterpillars, spiders, lizards, and small mammals. It hunts for its prey much like a cat does, creeping up on its victims and attacking quickly. The Grasshopper mouse nests in burrows that are abandoned by gophers, ground squirrels, or Deer mice. The Grasshopper mouse is most active at night.

Deer Mouse

The Deer mouse is often called the White-footed mouse, because like most deer, they have white hair around their paws. Its fur is brownish-gray on its back and white on its stomach. It has large ears. It measures 6–8" (15–20 cm) long. The Deer mouse inhabits a large amount of land area from Central America and up to the tree line of North America. It lives in mountain, desert, and swamp areas. It likes to nest beneath rocks, hollow logs, tree stumps, and in tunnels. The Deer mouse likes to go into people's homes to find soft materials such as cotton or wool to use in its nest. Berries, seeds, nuts, fruit, and insects make up a large part of its diet. When a Deer mouse becomes excited it will thump its feet rapidly on the ground making a drumming noise.

Mice Facts *(cont.)*

Cactus Mouse and Golden Mouse

The Cactus mouse and Golden mouse are close relatives of the Deer mouse. They are small mice with long tails—longer than their head and body. They have golden-brown fur on their backs and white fur on their stomachs and paws. The Cactus mouse likes the hot deserts of the southwestern United States and lives in low bushes and cacti. The Golden mouse builds its nest using grass and leaves in places as high as 15' (4.5 m) above the ground. The Golden mouse feeds on seeds and fruit.

Pocket Mouse

The Pocket mouse is relatively large in size—$4^1/_2$–5" (11.5–13 cm) long. It has tannish-brown outer fur and whitish fur underneath its belly. Its body has coarse hair. There are 20 or more species of Pocket mice, all similar in size and appearance. All Pocket mice are active at night. Some live in grassy areas along roads and fences; others are found in the dry areas along the Mississippi River. The Pocket mouse is able to carry its food using expandable pouches, called pockets, on the outside of its cheeks. Once inside the safety of its burrow, it forces out the seeds by pressing against the pouches with its front paws. It seldom drinks water. Instead, it gets moisture from the foods it eats.

Meadow or Western Jumping Mouse

The Meadow or Western Jumping mouse inhabits meadows and open spaces of most areas in North America from Alaska to the Atlantic Ocean and from North and South Carolina to Nevada. Its length is $3^1/_2$" (9 cm) and is yellowish-brown on its back and white on its stomach. It uses its long tail for balance and its long hind legs to spring into the air. It can leap distances of 5' (1.5 m) or more. Since it looks for food at night, it must be careful to not get eaten by bigger animals such as owls, snakes, weasels, and other predators when it is out in search of food. A Western Jumping mouse only uses its nest for winter hibernation. The rest of the year it sleeps and eats in a grassy area or under logs.

46

A Mice Map

See page 8 for directions.

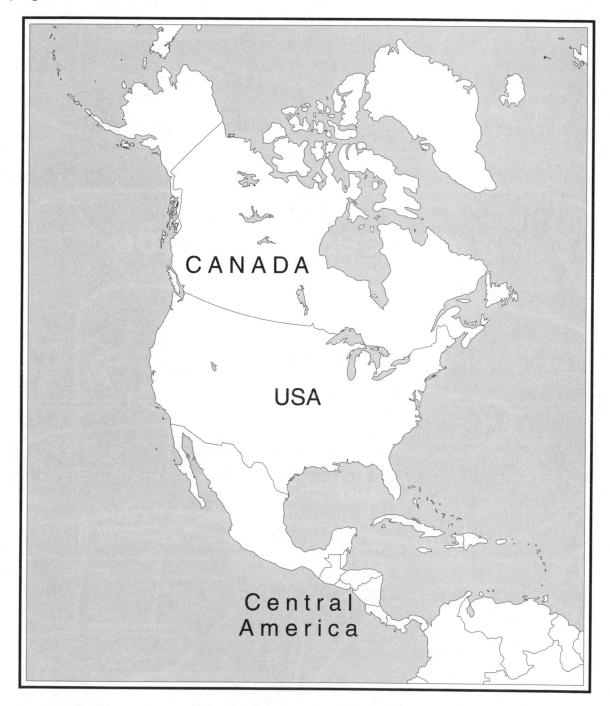

House Mouse	☐	Deer Mouse	☐	Cactus Mouse	☐
Harvest Mouse	☐	Pocket Mouse	☐	Golden Mouse	☐
Grasshopper Mouse	☐	Meadow or Western Jumping Mouse	☐		

Country Mouse

Use the map symbols in this story to help Country Mouse get back home on the map on page 49.

 started at the . He walked past the

and into the . From the he turned right to a new path and

walked past the  . He walked past the  and turned

left down the next path. He crossed over two  . He made a right

turn at the next corner. He crossed over one more . Country

Mouse is almost home! He ran past the  until he reached

his  .

48

A Map for Country Mouse

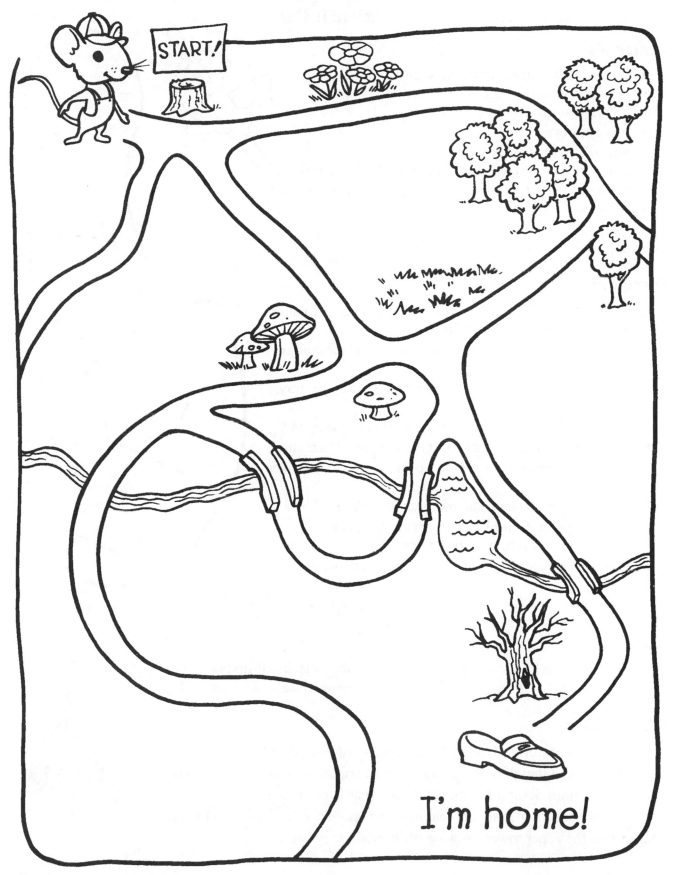

START!

I'm home!

Mouse Art

Pencil Pal

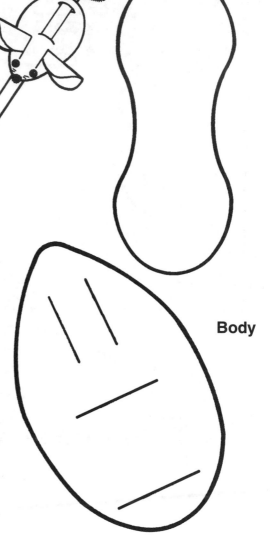

Ears

Body

Materials

- mouse body and ears pattern (right)
- gray felt squares
- pink felt scraps
- two craft eyes
- one ¼" (.6 cm) black pom pom
- four 1" (2.54 cm) lengths of black embroidery floss
- 2" (5 cm) length of gray or black pipe cleaner
- scissors
- glue
- pencil

Directions

1. Reproduce and cut out the mouse body and ears pattern from tagboard (to be used as tracing patterns).
2. Trace the body on the gray felt square and the ears on the pink felt.
3. Using the scissors, make two vertical slits in the gray, felt body as shown.
4. Make two horizontal slits near the front of the head.
5. Weave the ear pattern through the two horizontal slits.
6. Glue the eyes and nose (pom pom) on the mouse's face (as shown).
7. Curl the pipe cleaner tail and glue into place.
8. Using a permanent black felt tip marker, make whiskers and eyebrows on the gray felt.
9. Weave the pencil into place between the remaining slits.

Thumbprint Mice

Materials

- washable black-ink stamp pad
- white paper
- thin, black felt-tip pen
- paper towels

Directions

1. Using the stamp pad, push thumb gently onto inked pad.
2. Place inked thumb onto a sheet of white paper to create a mouse body.
3. Repeat until desired number of "mice" has been created.
4. Use the felt-tip pen to add features such as tails, eyes, noses, and whiskers.

(**Note:** Use the paper towels to wipe off hands if they get messy.)

Mouse Art *(cont.)*

Mousey Pet Rock

Materials

- one washed and dried, round and smooth small rock (per child)
- gray or white tempera paint
- paintbrush
- scissors
- gray or white felt
- pink felt
- craft glue
- six 2" (5 cm) black pipe cleaners
- 4" (10 cm) length of black pipe cleaner
- two wiggly, plastic craft eyes
- small, black button
- *Optional:* clear acrylic enamel spray paint

Directions

1. Paint the rock using the gray or white tempera paint; allow to dry. (*Optional:* Spray the painted rock with clear acrylic enamel spray paint; allow to dry.)
2. Cut out the ears free-hand from the gray or white felt; glue to the top of the mouse's head area.
3. Cut out smaller, free-form pink ears. Glue to the inside area of the gray or white felt ears.
4. Glue on the plastic eyes and button nose.
5. Glue the shorter pipe cleaners onto the mouse face for whiskers.
6. Using the remaining piece of pipe cleaner, bend it to form a tail and glue into place.

Mousey Stick Puppets

Materials

- Town Mouse and Country Mouse patterns, reproduced on white tagboard (pages 52 and 53)
- craft sticks
- crayons or felt markers
- scissors
- glue

Directions

1. Prepare the patterns in advance by having adults cut out the mice and clothing on pages 52 and 53. (**Note:** Do not cut off the clothing tabs.)
2. Distribute a set of mice and clothes to each child. Allow them to color the patterns.
3. Glue the mouse puppets to craft sticks.
4. Have the children hold the tabs down on the clothes and attach the clothes to the mouse bodies.

Stick Puppets

See the directions on page 51.

Stick Puppets *(cont.)*

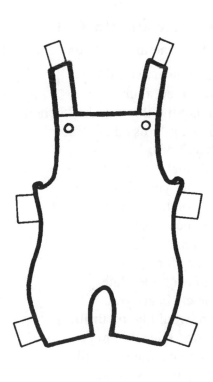 

Mouse-a-rific Songs

Songs composed by Michele McBride

Skitter! Skitter! Squeak!

(Sung to the tune of "The Farmer in the Dell")

He peered around the corner,
Then skittered through my feet.
He surely didn't seem afraid
He looked so cute and sweet!

(Refrain)

Skitter! Skitter! Squeak!
Skitter! Skitter! Squeak!
A little mouse is here to stay,
For me this is a treat!

He comes out every morning,
And dashes down the hall.
We've started quite a friendship,
Even though he's very small!

(Repeat refrain)

When the day comes to a close,
A tired mouse I see.
He plays the game I so enjoy,
I know he tries to please!

(Repeat refrain)

I'm glad this mouse moved in,
So nice to have a friend.
He's very welcome at my house,
May this dream never end!

Gray Mouse

(Sung to the tune of "Twinkle, Twinkle, Little Star")

Tiny, little, elfin mouse,
Scampered 'cross the floor.
Went into the pantry,
And under the door.
She crept very softly,
Not making a sound.
Some cheese to find,
Looking all around.
She skittered down the hallway,
Darted to the right.
Squeezed through a hole,
And vanished out of sight.

The Mice and the Cat

(Sung to the tune of "Ten Little Indians")

One mouse, two mice,
Three mice, four,
Scampering through the kitchen,
Whisking 'cross the floor.
Softly! Softly!
Don't make a sound.
Don't let your little feet
Patter on the ground.
Five mice, six mice,
Seven mice, eight,
Sniffing for a wee lunch,
Crumbs on the plate.
If the cat hears you,
There would be no thrill,
For nine mice, ten mice,
Who come along at will.
One mouse, two mice,
Count them up to ten,
When the meal is over,
Back into the den.
Little mice be careful,
When you want to roam.
For if you should wake him,
He'll chase you back home!

Mouse-a-rific Songs *(cont.)*

Five Little Mice Action Song

(Sung to the tune of "Five Little Pumpkins")

Five little mice, *(Hold up five fingers.)*
Peeking 'round a door, *(Encircle each eye with thumb and forefinger.)*
One crept outside, *(Make your fingers do a walk.)*
And then there were four. *(Hold up four fingers.)*
Four little mice, *(Hold up four fingers.)*
Playful as could be, *(Dance with your fingers in the air.)*
One stopped to rest awhile, *(Rest your head in hands.)*
And then there were three. *(Hold up three fingers.)*
Three little mice, *(Hold up three fingers.)*
Wondering what to do, *(Put forefinger under chin as if you are thinking.)*
One scampered 'cross the floor, *(Scamper away with your fingers.)*
And then there were two. *(Hold up two fingers.)*
Two little mice, *(Hold up two fingers.)*
Basking in the sun, *(Put hands at the back of your head and lean back.)*
One wanted shade, *(Put your hand up to shade your eyes.)*
And then there was one. *(Hold up one finger.)*
One little mouse, *(Hold up one finger.)*
Tired from his fun, *(Lay your head in your hands.)*
Vanished in his mouse den, *(Move head back and forth like you're looking for something.)*
And then there were none! *(Hold thumb and forefinger together to form a zero.)*
No little mice, *(Use thumb and forefinger to show zero.)*
To scamper and play, *(Scamper away with your fingers.)*
The bright sun is setting, *(Make a circle with your hands above your head and then move circle downward in front of your body.)*
It's the end of the day! *(Fold hands in front of you.)*

A Wee Little Gray Mouse

(Sung to the tune of "Itsy Bitsy Spider")

A wee, little, gray mouse,
Creeping 'cross the floor.
Under the table,
And out through the door.
Skitter, skitter, squeak, squeak,
Pattering on the ground.
Very, very softly,
Don't make a sound.
Sniff the air for danger,
Careful as you roam.
Nibbling on some sweet seeds,
Now hurry, hurry home.

Peering very carefully,
Listening for a sound.
At the sign of trouble,
To the den will bound.
When the sun is setting,
Scamper for the door.
Watch for the sly cat,
Dash 'cross the floor.
Safe in a warm den,
Away from any harm.
Out again to see the world,
At the light of the dawn.

   #2365 Thematic Unit—Mice

Mouse Recipes

Mouse Salad

Ingredients

- 1 large lettuce leaf
- 2 slices of banana
- ½ of a maraschino cherry
- 2 raisins
- 1 canned pear half
- 1 slice cheese, cut into slivers

Directions

Arrange the ingredients on a washed and dried lettuce leaf, using the pear half for the mouse's "body," the banana slices for the "ears," the raisins for the "eyes," the cherry for the "nose," and the cheese slivers for the "whiskers" and the "tail."

Squeaky Mouse Cookies

Ingredients

- 1 cup (225 g) butter or margarine, softened
- 1 egg
- 1 teaspoon (5 mL) vanilla extract
- small, red cinnamon candies
- thin, black licorice strings, cut into 2" (5 cm) lengths
- 1 cup (225 g) packed brown sugar
- 1 teaspoon (5 mL) almond extract
- 3½ cups (790 g) all-purpose flour
- 1 cup (225 g) shelled peanuts
- ½ cup (100 g) raisins

Directions

In a large mixing bowl, cream the butter and brown sugar; beat in the egg, vanilla, and almond extract. Gradually add the flour; mix well. Cover and chill the dough for 1 hour. Shape the dough into 1" (2.4 cm) balls, pinching the front of each ball slightly to form a small nose. Place the mouse cookies on an ungreased baking sheet. Add two peanut halves for ears, two raisins for the eyes and one small, red candy for the nose. Poke a small hole in the dough for the tail (to be added later) with a toothpick. Bake at 325 degrees F (160 degrees C) for 12 minutes or until the edges are lightly browned. Remove from the oven; cool on wire racks. Insert the licorice pieces for tails. Makes about 5 dozen.

Mint Tea

Ingredients

- 1 quart (1 L) cold water
- ¼ cup (50 g) fresh mint leaves
- 4 tea bags
- granulated sugar

Directions

Boil the water over high heat. Remove from heat; add the tea bags. Cover and allow to steep for about five minutes. Remove the tea bags. Sweeten to taste. Serve in cups with a sprig of mint leaves floating on top of each serving.

Have a Cheesy Time!

Plan a mouse-a-rific party and invite parents, administrators, and other classes to join in the fun.

Create a Mouse-a-rific Atmosphere

1. Reproduce and distribute the invitations (page 73) for your children to cut out, decorate, and deliver.

2. If you have not already done so, create a mousey entrance to your room (page 18, Setting the Stage, #2).

3. Display child-created art projects (pages 50 and 51) as decorations around the room.

4. Prepare the *Belling the Cat* choral play (pages 64 and 65).

5. Have the children record the Mouse-a-rific Songs (pages 54 and 55) on a cassette tape and have the songs playing as the guests arrive. (An alternative would be to have the children make up original song lyrics to familiar tunes.)

6. Plan a mousey snack table using the treats listed on page 56. Easy snack alternatives may be bowls of such food items as nuts, seeds, and dried fruit.

Consider these Mouse-a-rific Activities

1. Have the children help you prepare five "sensation stations." Each station will feature a different sense—see, hear, smell, taste, or feel. Place the children into teams of three or four. Have them gather and prepare the necessary materials for the senses stations. (The senses activities may be chosen from those featured on pages 59–63.) You may want to ask parents or other adults to assist in the setting up and supervision of the stations. On the day of the mouse-a-rific party, have your guests rotate from station to station based on a predetermined time and rotation schedule (page 58).

2. Have the children retell the *Town Mouse Country Mouse* tale using stick puppets (pages 51–53).

3. Copy the Mousey Poems and Chants (page 23) and the Mouse-a-rific Songs (pages 54 and 55) on large paper and have everyone join in the reading and singing fun.

4. Play the Cat and Mice game (page 8, #9).

Sense Stations

Preparation

Gather and prepare the necessary materials as outlined for each station (pages 59–63). Divide the guests into five teams: A, B, C, D, and E. (**Note:** If you have chosen to have your children rotate through the stations during the rotation time rather than guests, you may want to enlist the help of adult volunteers to be leaders at each station.)

Rotate through the Stations

Each station takes approximately eight minutes to complete. If you use all the suggested stations, it will take approximately one hour to rotate your children or guests through all five. Plan to ring a bell or blow a whistle at the end of each station session to signal the need to clean up and rotate to the next station.

Station One	Station Two	Station Three	Station Four	Station Five
A	B	C	D	E
E	A	B	C	D
D	E	A	B	C
C	D	E	A	B
B	C	D	E	A

Sense Stations *(cont.)*

Station One: Mice-Peeking Pictures (See)

Preparation

1. Reproduce the squeaky-mouse head pattern (page 67) 10 times.

2. Color, cut out, and glue each reproduced squeaky mouse head to the front of a file folder.

3. Using a box cutter or sharp razor blade, cut out the mice's eye sockets and inner ear areas. Be certain that you cut through both the mouse face and the front half of the glued-onto file folder.

4. Inside each prepared folder, on the back half of the folder, glue a colorful picture (calendar pictures work well). When the folders are closed, parts of the glued-down pictures should now be visible through the mice's eye and inner-ear openings.

5. Place the prepared folders, along with drawing paper, pencils, and crayons, in the station area.

Activity

The leader holds up one of the file folders. The children/guests take turns asking the leader yes-or-no-questions to try to determine what the hidden picture is. Depending on time limits, have each child/guest illustrate what they perceive the picture to be using the drawing paper, pencils, and crayons before revealing it. Repeat with as many file-folder, mice-peeking pictures as time allows.

Sense Stations *(cont.)*

Station Two: Mouse Messages (Hear)

Preparation

Write the following messages on 5" x 7" (13 cm x 18 cm) cards:

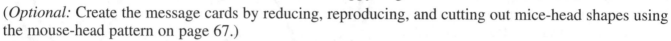

- Town Mouse went for a walk in the country.
- Country Mouse loved the smell of cheese.
- Town Mouse and Country Mouse changed places.
- Country Mouse caught his tail in the breadbox.
- Country Mouse landed on a warm, furry bundle.
- Town Mouse felt a drop of rain on his head.
- Town Mouse was proud of his eye-catching bright new jacket.
- Town Mouse and Country Mouse were so happy to get back to their own homes.

(*Optional:* Create the message cards by reducing, reproducing, and cutting out mice-head shapes using the mouse-head pattern on page 67.)

Activity

Have the children/guests sit close together in a circle so they can easily whisper into each other's ears. The leader shuffles the message cards and places them face down (text not showing). A child/guest picks up the top card and passes it to the leader. The leader whispers what the message says into the ear of one of the team members. (Each team member must listen carefully because the mouse message cannot be repeated a second time in someone's "already-heard-the-message" ear.) The team member then turns and whispers to the next person what he or she thinks they heard. The message continues around from ear to ear in a whispering-in-the-ear fashion until the message reaches the last person. This team member then shares aloud what the mouse message was. What a surprise to hear how the message changed! (**Note:** This activity is similar to the classic party game called Telephone.)

Station Three: The Nose Knows (Smell)

Materials: hammer; nails; 10 baby food jars with lids; contact paper; 10 cotton balls; 10 pungent-smelling items (e.g., peppermint, orange, cinnamon extract, peanut butter, cocoa, coffee, pickle juice, garlic clove, onion, pineapple, banana, chili); pictures of the chosen smelly items, mounted onto 3" x 3" (8 cm x 8 cm) cardboard squares (some smells you have chosen may appear on page 62).

Preparation

Punch a hole in each lid with the hammer and nail. Place a cotton ball in each jar.

Cover the outside of the glass jars with contact paper or spray paint so the glass cannot be seen through.

Add a "smell" to each jar. Screw the lids back onto the jars. On the bottom of each jar, label each jar's contents.

Activity

The leader asks the team members if they think they can guess what is in each jar using just the sense of smell. The leader shows the 10 pictures and asks them to smell each jar and match the pictures to the correct jar. When the children/guests think they have them matched correctly, have the leader reveal the answers by checking the bottom of each jar. If time allows, have the children/guests try again after having the jars thoroughly mixed up.

Sense Stations *(cont.)*

Station Four: Name That Taste (Taste)

Preparation

Create and display a chart with three columns labeled: sweet, sour, and salty.

Activity

Read the three descriptive words listed on the chart. Discuss each word briefly. Give each child a paper plate containing a food item from each "S" category, such as:

- sweet—candy, sugar cube, soda pop, chocolate, cookie
- sour—lemon, grapefruit, vinegar, unsweetened fruit punch
- salty—pretzels, potato chips, salt, peanuts, pickles

Have the children/guests try their three food samples and talk to each other to decide how they want to classify these foods. List their choices on the chart paper with a marker. If time allows, pass out another plate containing three new food samples and try a second round of "Name that Taste."

Station Five: "Touchy-Feely" Game (Tactile Feel)

Materials

- reproduced Touch Cards (page 63), on heavy paper
- textured materials (two of each), such as:

    rough—sandpaper, thin scouring pad, bark from a tree
    smooth—aluminum foil, paper, ribbon
    bumpy—wallpaper, corrugated cardboard, dried seeds
    hard—wood, metal, rock, macaroni pieces
    soft—fabric, cotton balls, yarn, velvet

- marker
- scissors
- glue
- blindfolds

Preparations

Cut out the reproduced card sets. Glue like items onto two matching-text cards.

(**Note:** To make more matching sets, simply reproduce additional copies of page 63.)

Directions

Provide every two players with five sets of prepared Touch cards. Have one player blindfold his or her partner. This player then lays down the matching sets in a concentration-game array (with the textures facing up). The blindfolded player then touches the cards and tries to make matches. When he or she has matched all of the sets correctly, the players switch roles.

Sense Station Cards

banana

chili

peppermint

orange

cinnamon

peanuts

chocolate

coffee

pickle

garlic

onion

pineapple

Touch Cards

soft	soft
hard	hard
bumpy	bumpy
smooth	smooth
rough	rough

Belling the Cat Choral Play

Characters
- Narrator
- Father Mouse
- Mother Mouse
- Children
- Aunt Mouse
- Uncle Mouse
- Cat

Narrator: Once upon a time there lived a family of mice,
In a grand, old house that was quiet and nice.
It was a happy life, with time to play and chat,
But everything changed when along came Cat.
He was big and scary, sleek and furry.
He had all the mice scurrying in a hurry.
Now quiet please—no moving this way or that,
And I'll tell you the story of *Belling the Cat*.

Father: Whew! That was close. I was nearly a feast,
For that pu-r-r-fectly, terrible, four-legged beast!

Mother: We can hardly snatch a crumb of bread,
When up pops the meanest, the furriest, cat-y head.
Cat is everywhere. We just don't have a chance.
We must keep up watching with a backward glance.

Children: He runs around with his green eyes shining,
Before you know it, he has thoughts of dining!
We always have to quickly run home,
That cat is crafty and likes to roam.

Aunt: I'm still sh-a-k-ing from yesterday's scare.
His breath was hot and it warmed the air.

Belling The Cat Choral Play *(cont.)*

Cat: Meow! Meow! May I join in the fun?
A mouse party should be for everyone.
Mousies, mousies, won't you come out?
I promise to be kind—without a doubt.

Aunt: Don't fall for those cute, little kitty tricks.
His claws are ready and his tongue he licks.
Oh dear, my nerves will soon give out,
That cat is such a pest, without a doubt.

Uncle: Our lives are precious, we will confess.
What can we do? We're in such a mess.

Father: I have a clever plan to keep us free.
A bell for Cat, loud and shiny.

Mother: A great idea, but what do we do,
To solve our problem and be safe, too?

Uncle: I'm too old and very slow at that.
I can't possibly tie a bell on Cat.

Children: We can't do it, we are much too small.
An older mouse must answer this call.

Uncle: A volunteer is what we need,
To do this bold and risky deed.
To creep up on Cat and gently place
A loud jingle bell all covered in lace.

Father: The only way to trick that cat,
Is to catch him asleep on his little mat.

Narrator: So our story ends—a plan in place,
The mice needed to win this special race.
Win they did. They belled that cat.
And now they are safe, and that is that!

Senses Bulletin Board

Our Five Senses

This bulletin board display utilizes the Squeaky Mouse patterns found on pages 67–69. Reproduce the mouse body parts onto white or light-gray tagboard. For each mouse, cut out the pattern pieces and use paper fasteners or glue to put the mouse together. (**Note:** You will need to position each sense's mouse so that the pointing finger/hand directs your eyes to that sense area.) Display on the prepared bulletin-board background or in the hallway. Reproduce onto yellow construction paper a total of five cheese wedges (using the pattern on page 70); cut out the wedges and label them respectively: See, Smell, Taste, Hear, Feel.

As an introduction to the senses unit, gather the children around the prepared bulletin board. Have them identify what the first mouse is pointing to (its eye). When we see things, our eyes are using the sense called: see. Have a child attach the See cheese wedge under the appropriate mouse. Continue this process with the remaining four senses. If the children already have an initial awareness of the five senses, allow them to play a more interactive role and choose a wedge first and decide which mouse is displaying that sense.

To use the bulletin board in another interactive way, place questions/math facts onto reproduced cheese wedges and information/answers onto the mice's bodies. For example, to review addition problems to 10, label the five mice with a specific sum (3, 5, 7, 8, 10) and then on the cheese wedges write the number problems (1 + 2, 2 + 3, 2 + 5, 4 + 4, 5 + 5). Have your children match the cheese wedges to the correct mouse.

Squeaky Mouse

See pages 7 and 66 for directions for this activity.

Squeaky Mouse *(cont.)*

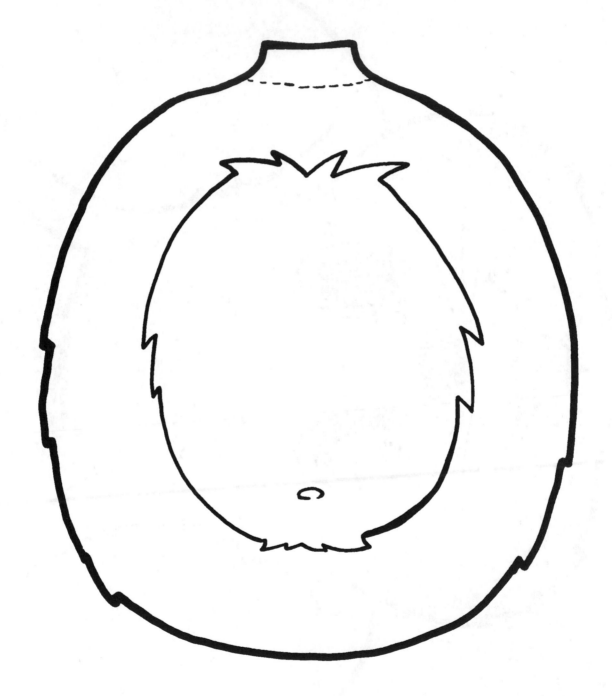

68

Squeaky Mouse (cont.)

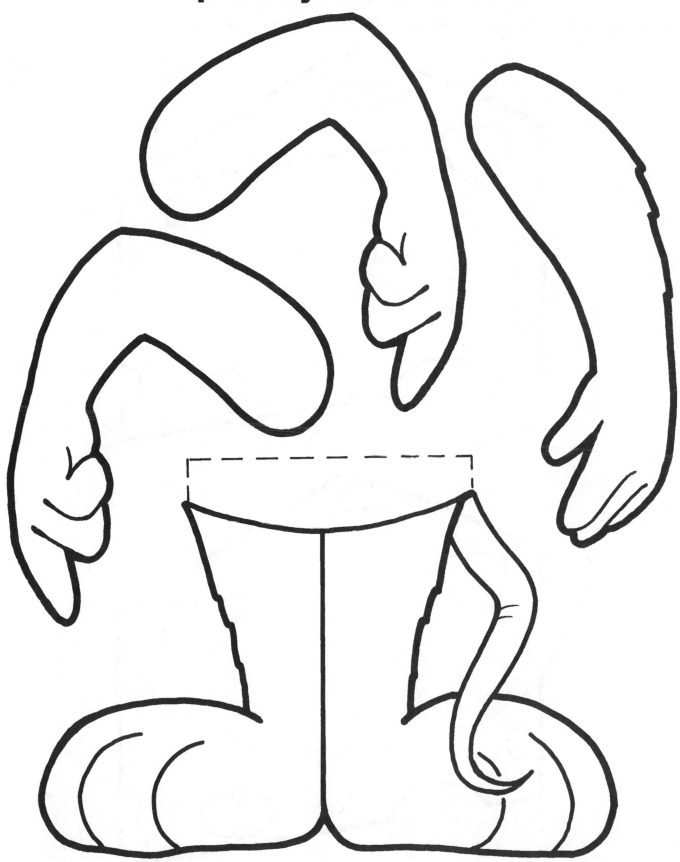

Cheese-Wedge Pattern

See pages 7 and 66 for directions for this activity.

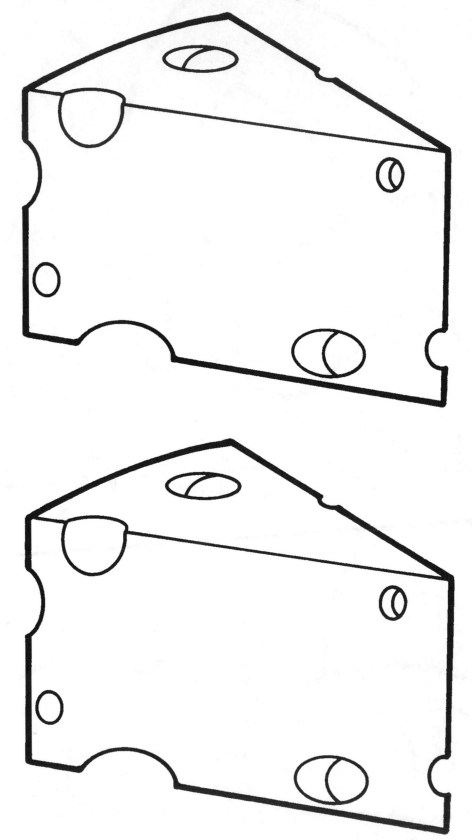

Mice Learning Center

Learning center activities and materials should review, reinforce, and enrich concepts and skills previously taught. The activities should also be designed to address individual differences in your children's learning styles. The learning center can be designed for individual or cooperative use.

For success in your mice learning center, consider the following:

- decorate the center with mouse illustrations or photos
- develop activities that can be completed cooperatively or individually
- create language activities that include some of the writing ideas (pages 24–26), word search and vocabulary building (page 27) and songs (pages 54 and 55)
- provide facts about mice (pages 74–76), as well as display Food Chain Chart (page 77)
- display the Mousey Poems and Chants (page 23) and the Mouse-a-rific Songs (pages 54 and 55)
- provide resource materials such as mice books (Bibliography, page 79), pencils, paper, art supplies, and game materials as needed to complete your created activities

Mousey Nest

Set up a comfortable and quiet poetry or story area that resembles a mouse's nest. Use blankets, pillows, or bean bag chairs to form the nest. Add a basket filled with mice books (Bibliography, page 79). If desired, place stuffed mouse toys in the nest area for your children to cuddle up to.

Reproduce the bookmark (page 73) on tagboard. Give a child a bookmark after they have read one of the books available in the mousey nest basket of books.

Mousey Awards

You are Mouse-a-rific!

Teacher

Date

A Big Cheese Award!

to

for

Teacher

Date

72

Bookmark and Invitation

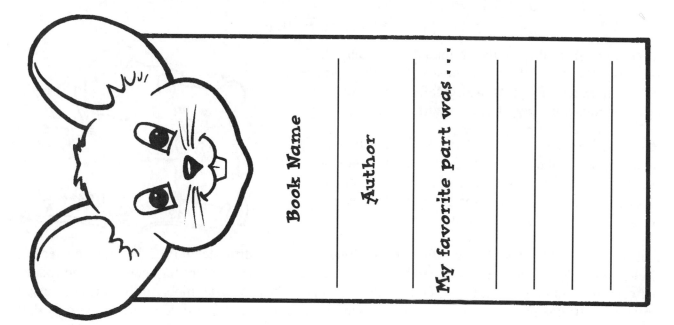

Book Name

Author

My favorite part was . . .

You are invited!

Please come to our Mouse-a-rific Party.

Date: _____

Time: _____

Place: _____

Facts about Mice

Rodent Family

Mice come from the family of gnawing animals called *rodents*. These include rats, hamsters, gerbils, lemmings, voles, and mice. Rodents are actually distant relatives of beavers, muskrats, porcupines, squirrels, and chipmunks.

Rodents' bodies are usually 3–6" (8–15 cm) long and their tails are usually 3–4" (8–10 cm) long. Their short, soft fur can be gray, white, black, or brown in color. They have pointed snouts, small round, black eyes, rounded ears, and long, thin tails.

Rodents have two types of teeth. Incisors are long, chisel-like front teeth used for gnawing seeds, shells, and wood. Flat, hard back teeth, called cheek teeth, are important for chewing. The space between the front and back teeth is called the *diastema*. This space is important because some species suck their cheeks into this space and close off the mouth, making it possible for them to gnaw shells or wood without swallowing gnawed pieces. A rodent's front teeth grow throughout its lifetime.

Mice use their claws for grooming, scratching, climbing, and fighting. When climbing up and down ropes, branches, or walls, their claws dig into the surfaces. When necessary, their tails aid in climbing and balancing.

Mice Are Mammals

Mice belong to the class of animals called *mammals*. These vertebrates (back-boned animals) produce live young and the newborn babies drink milk from their mother's mammary glands. The gestation for mice is approximately 20 to 27 days. The newborn babies are no bigger than a thimble and they weigh less then the weight of a feather! Mice babies are weak and helpless at birth and need constant care and support from their mothers. Their eyes are closed; they have no fur, and are deaf and blind. After about two weeks, they develop a fur coat and open their eyes. A group of baby mice is called a *litter*. A female mouse may produce five to ten litters a year. Each litter may have up to 12 young. After a month of life, a mouse is fully-grown and is ready to reproduce.

Food for Mice

Mice eat a variety of foods. They always seem to be in search of food, but they actually require little food to live. Many people think that a mouse's favorite food is cheese, but that is not true. Mice that live indoors eat scraps or crumbs of any leftover food. Mice will also eat paper, candles, glue, and even soap. Indoor mice are known for damaging many household belongings. Mice droppings can also damage nibbled foods and render them unfit for human consumption. When mice live outdoors, they eat mainly seeds and fruit, but they also eat plants and berries. Some species of mice enjoy a diet of insects, worms, and small mammals. Like rats, pigeons, flies, and ants, mice are called *commensals* because they eat foods left by the "original eater," and the owner's dwelling quite often shelters them.

Facts About Mice (cont.)

Homes for Mice

Mice live wherever they can find food and shelter. They make their nests in barns, attics, basements, fields, and underground burrows. They often line their nests with scraps of yarn, paper, cloth, leaves, or grass. They do not always live in "clean" places. Mice can often be found living in garbage dumps, condemned buildings, and manure piles. Indoor mice usually live behind the house's walls, in between attic beams or exterior bricks, in dark cellars, and under the floorboards. Outdoor mice live in fields and woodlands and generally live in burrows under the ground. The network of burrows has an  inconspicuous surface entrance that is kept blocked during the day. The underground shelter has a tunnel system that includes individual sleeping, nesting, and food storage chambers. Some types of mice also have been known to live in clumps of grass or bushes, rather than in deep, underground burrows.

Kinds of Mice

There are hundreds of kinds of mice and they live in most parts of the world. Mice can be found in civilized areas as well as in remote mountains, woodlands, or desert areas.

The word mouse means "thief" and comes from an ancient Sanskrit Asian language. Scientists believe that the House mouse originated in Asia. House mice later spread from Asia to Europe and eventually were brought to North and South America on the early English-Spanish sailing ships during the sixteenth century.

Mice are Territorial

Mice sleep and hunt in an area known as their territory. They are easily excited and agitated if a strange mouse enters their territory. They will not hesitate to chase other mice away. Mice will often tolerate other animals sharing their territory but not another mouse. Mice mark their territory with urine or droppings that give off a pungent smell. Unfortunately, it's hard to get rid of these territorial smells in attics or basements.

Mice Enemies

Almost every predator is an enemy of the mouse. Predators include cats, dogs, coyotes, foxes, snakes, owls, eagles, and hawks. Rats and other mice can also be enemies. Man is probably the worst enemy of the House mouse, as is the man-made invention—the mousetrap. Mice easily fall prey to the smell of cheese or peanut butter attached to the mousetrap's wire. House mice may be fortunate to live as long as a year in an attic or basement, but outdoor mice survive only two or three months. Mice avoid their enemies by constantly hiding and they seldom wander far from their nests. Mice try to keep concealed by moving quietly under furniture, boxes, or around plants. They rarely run out into the open spaces unless they feel a need to scamper away quickly. Although mice can swim, they avoid water.

Facts About Mice *(cont.)*

Mice Are Nocturnal

Animals and birds that are active and hunt at night are *nocturnal*. Most mice are nocturnal. Mice have poor vision but know their territory and can find their way in the dark by using their keen sense of smell. At night meadows and woodlands are active with predators such as owls, bats, foxes, and raccoons in search of small rodents such as mice. Therefore, even in the dark, a mouse must be consistently cautious.

Do All Mice Hibernate?

In spite of what people think, not all mice hibernate. Some mice remain active during the winter months. They collect seeds in their stretchy cheek pouches and store them in chambers near their nest. Mice that do not hibernate spend the wintertime huddled together in groups to stay warm. These underground dwelling mice travel back and forth through their tunnels during the coldest months of the year.

Some types of mice, such as the Jumping mice, develop a layer of fat in the fall by eating extra food and enter a deep sleep until spring. Extra fat protects the mice from cold and provides what little energy their bodies need. Mice curl into a ball and their body temperature drops. Their body functions such as heart rate and breathing slow down as they enter a deep sleep. Occasionally, hibernating mice wake up to eat their stored food. The mice then go back to sleep and continue their hibernation.

Safety Precautions with Mice

In recent years, the Deer mouse has become a carrier of a disease that can make humans sick and can even cause death. The fumes from the infected mouse droppings, if breathed by humans, can make them ill and sometimes result in death. This rare disease is called *Hantavirus Pulmonary Syndrome*. Deer mice are most commonly found in Central America and up into the treeline (the northern limit of tree growth) or timberline (the altitude at which timber ceases to grow) in North America.

Mice as Part of the Food Chain

Plants and animals live together in harmony in order to keep the balance of nature in check. The diagram (page 77) shows the essential part a mouse plays in keeping the food chain intact.

Mice for Experimental Purposes

Scientists often study mice to learn about their behavior under controlled conditions. They are interested in why mice act as they do. Mice used in experiments are usually of the House mouse species. Scientists look for ways to keep people well or cure illnesses by using white laboratory mice in experiments to discover new cures for diseases. Using mice for experimental purposes is a sensitive issue. Many animal activists are not comfortable with the use of mice in this experimental manner.

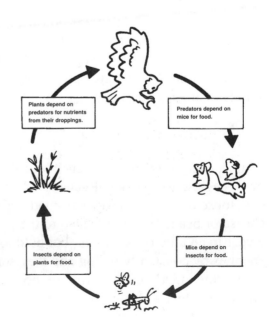

Plants depend on predators for nutrients from their droppings.

Predators depend on mice for food.

Mice depend on insects for food.

Insects depend on plants for food.

Food Chain Chart

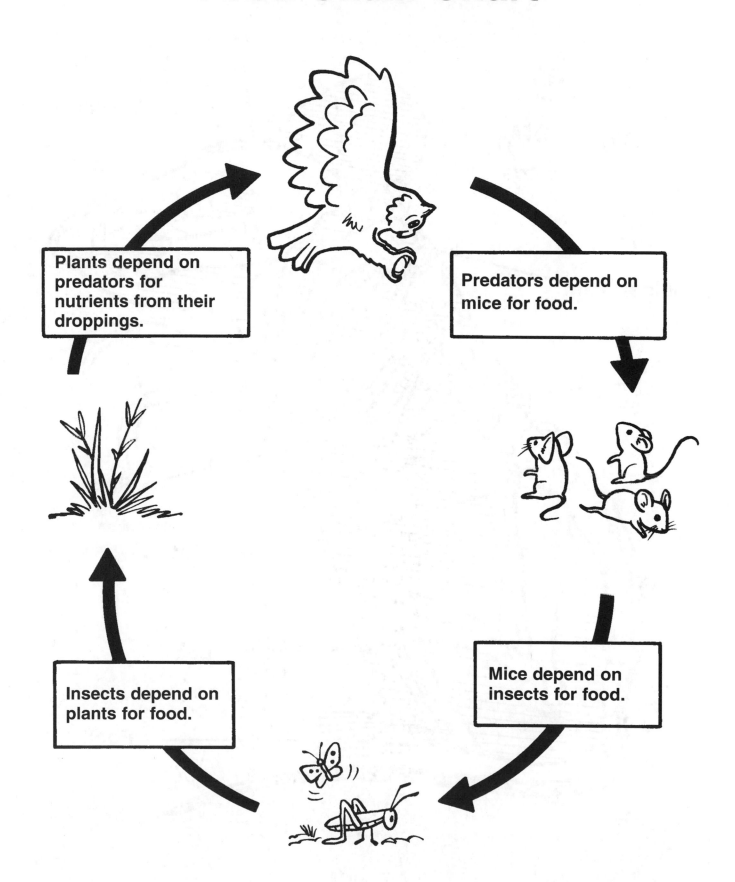

Plants depend on predators for nutrients from their droppings.

Predators depend on mice for food.

Insects depend on plants for food.

Mice depend on insects for food.

Mouse Skeleton

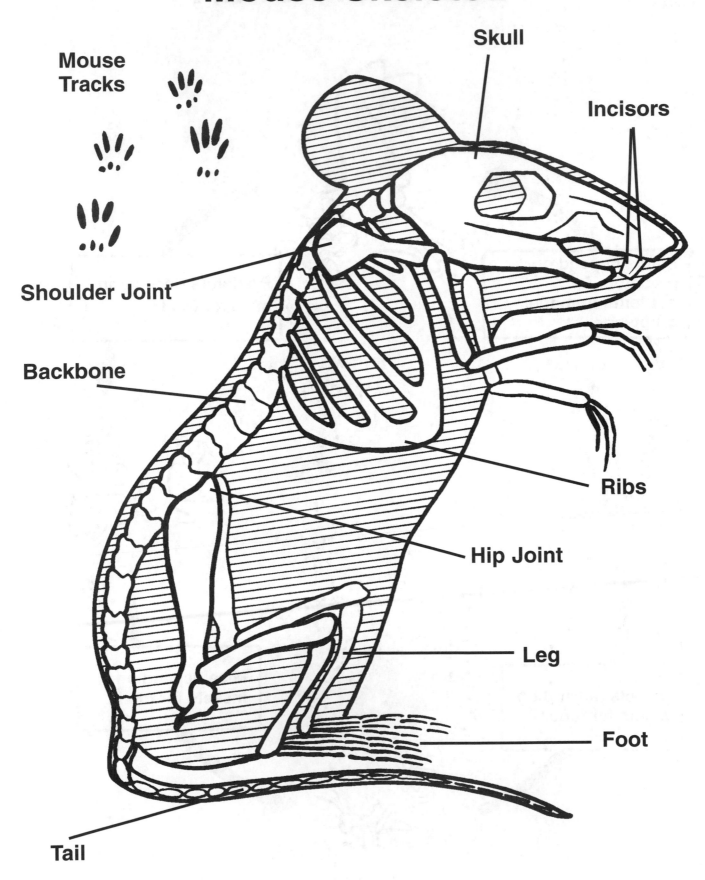

Skull

Incisors

Mouse
Tracks

Shoulder Joint

Backbone

Ribs

Hip Joint

Leg

Foot

Tail

Bibliography

Fiction

Aesop. *City Mouse Country Mouse.* Scholastic, 1987.

Barber, Antonia. *Satchelmouse and the Dinosaurs.* Children's Press, 1973.

Berson, Harold. *A Moose is Not a Mouse.* Crown, 1987.

Bluth, Brad. *Siegfried's Silent Night.* Children's Press, 1991.

Brandenburg, Franz. *Nice New Neighbors.* Scholastic, 1977.

Bunting, Eve. *The Mother's Day Mice.* Clarion, 1986.

Carle, Eric. *Do You Want to be My Friend?* Crowell, 1971.

Cauley, L. B. *The Town Mouse and the Country Mouse.* Putnam, 1984.

Claret, Maria. *Melissa Mouse's Birthday Surprise.* Methuen, 1986.

Cleary, Beverly. *Runaway Ralph.* Listening Library, 1983.

Cosgrove, Stephen. *Little Mouse on the Prairie.* Price-Stern-Sloan, 1980.

Craig, Helen. *The Town Mouse and the Country Mouse.* Walker, 1992.

Crust, Linda. *Melvin's Cold Feet.* Gareth Stevens, 1991.

Dungan, Riana. *A Tale of Ten Town Mice.* Rourke, 1982.

Edwards, Pamela. *Livingstone Mouse.* Harper Collins, 1996.

Forward, Tony. *The Christmas Mouse.* Anderson, 1996.

Gelman, Rita. *Cats and Mice.* Scholastic, 1990.

Hurd, Thatcher. *Little Mouse's Big Valentine.* Harper, 1990.

Ivimey, John W. *The Complete Story of the Three Blind Mice.* Clarion, 1987.

Iwamura, Kazuo. *The Fourteen Forest Mice and the Harvest Moon Watch.* Gareth Stevens, 1991.

Iwamura, Kazuo. *The Fourteen Forest Mice and the Spring Meadow Picnic.* Gareth Stevens, 1991.

Iwamura, Kazuo. *The Fourteen Forest Mice and the Summer Laundry Day.* Gareth Stevens, 1991.

Iwamura, Kazuo. *The Fourteen Forest Mice and the Winter Sledding Day.* Gareth Stevens, 1991.

Kellogg, Steven. *The Island of the Skog.* Dial, 1973.

Kraus, Robert. *Another Mouse to Feed.* Simon & Schuster, 1980.

Kraus, Robert. *Come Out and Play, Little Mouse.* Greenwillow, 1987.

Kraus, Robert. *Where Are You Going, Little Mouse?* Mulberry, 1989.

Kraus, Robert. *Whose Mouse Are You?* Aladdin, 1986.

Kumin, Maxine. *Joey and the Birthday Present.* McGraw-Hill, 1971.

Larrick, Nancy. *Mice Are Nice.* Philomel, 1990.

Lawson, Robert. *Ben and Me.* Little Brown, 1939.

Lionni, Leo. *Alexander and the Wind-up Mouse.* Knopf, 1969.

Lionni, Leo. *Frederick.* Knopf, 1973.

Mahy, Margaret. *The Pop Group.* Children's Press, 1990.

McBratney, Sam. *The Dark at the Top of the Stairs.* Candlewick, 1995.

McCully, Emily Arnold. *First Snow.* Harper Press, 1985.

Miller, Edna. *Mousekin's Golden House.* Prentice-Hall, 1964.

O'Brien, Robert C. *Mrs. Frisby and the Rats of Nimh.* Anthenum, 1986.

Polushkin, Maria. *Mother, Mother, I Want Another.* Crown, 1978.

Preller, James. *Wake Me in Spring.* Scholastic, 1994.

Ross, Tony. *Hugo and Oddsock.* Rourke, 1982.

Schecter, Ellen. *The Town Mouse and the Country Mouse.* Bantam, 1995.

Schmidt, Bernard. *Our Friend the Writer.* Garret, 1989.

Steig, William. *Abel's Island.* Farrar, Straus and Giroux, 1985.

Stevens, Janet. *The Town Mouse and The Country Mouse.* Holiday House, 1987.

Stone, Bernard. *Emergency Mouse.* Rourke, 1995.

Wenning, Elizabeth. *The Christmas Mouse.* Holt Rinehart, 1959.

White, E.B. *Stuart Little.* Harper, 1945.

Bibliography *(cont.)*

Fiction *(cont.)*

Winter, Yvonne. *Mr. Brown's Magnificent Apple Tree*. Scholastic, 1987.
Young, Ed. *Seven Blind Mice*. Philomel, 1992.

Nonfiction

Harrison, Virginia. *The World of Mice*. Gareth Stevens, 1988.
Jeunesse, Gallimard. *The Mouse*. Moonlight, 1992.
Royston, Angela. *Mouse*. Scholastic, 1992.
Sheehan, Angela. *The Mouse*. Warwick, 1985.

Video Recordings

Sony Music Entertainment. *Forest Animals*. Sony Music Inc., 1994.

Magazine

The Rat Mouse Gazette
www.rmca.org/Gazette/
A bi-monthly magazine that features articles on mice and rats. It is an informative, helpful, and interesting site.

Materials

Story Aprons (page 6)

Book Props
16825 S. Chapin Way
Lake Oswego, OR 97034
800-636-5314

Puppet Pals

J A L Enterprises (Annabelle Redman)
1138 Forestbrook Drive
Penticton, BC Canada V2A 2G5